Praise for *Pastori*

"I know dozens of pastors who want and need to take a time apart from their ministries to renew their energies for the tasks of Christian leadership. Yet many of them do not know how to contend for, plan, and take renewal leave. Greg Pimlott gives both the theological and personal justification and practical, step-by-step guidance you need for renewal of your ministry."

Will Willimon
Professor, Practice of Christian Ministry, Duke Divinity School
United Methodist Bishop, retired
author of *Accidental Preacher: A Memoir*

"Greg Pimlott has written a very encouraging book for pastors and congregations who are considering a renewal leave as a shared adventure between the pastor and congregation. Combining winsome storytelling with practical advice, he is a trustworthy guide for congregations and pastors that want to dream together about renewal in the immediate and long terms. Highly recommended!"

Robert Saler
Director, Lilly Endowment Clergy Renewal Programs

"*Pastoral Pause* is an essential read for pastors confronting burnout and seeking renewal. With heartfelt anecdotes and practical advice, Pimlott offers a roadmap for planning and executing a rejuvenating sabbatical. This book not only validates the spiritual necessity of taking breaks but also provides the tools and insights for sustaining effective ministry."

Cameron Trimble
CEO, Convergence
author of *Piloting Church* and *Searching for the Sacred*

"For the weary pastor plagued by over-work, depleting inner reserves, and vocational burnout, Pimlott offers a practical guide for an intentional and holy renewal leave. *Pastoral Pause* is a timely gift to pastors and congregations committed to life-giving leaves and healthy returns."

Rev. Mark Feldmeir,
Senior Pastor of St. Andrew UMC, Highlands Ranch, Colorado
author of *Life After God*

"These pages are truly filled with inspiration and practical plans for renewing lives tattered and worn out from the well-intentioned practices of ministry. Greg's perspective provides a timely and encouraging word for pastors to find healthy and realistic responses to the subtle and not-so-subtle demands of church leadership."

Bishop Julius C. Trimble
Resident Bishop, Indiana Conference of the UMC
author of *10 Reasons I Am a Methodist*

Pastoral Pause

A PRACTICAL GUIDE TO RENEWAL LEAVE

GREG PIMLOTT

UPPER
ROOM BOOKS®
NASHVILLE

ISBN: 978-0-8358-2056-1
Epub ISBN: 978-0-8358-2057-8

Cover design: Faceout Studio
Interior design: PerfecType, Nashville, TN

To Julie
my partner in life, love, and ministry,
with deep gratitude to God.

CONTENTS

Part Four: The Pastor Returns

Appendix

†††

PART ONE

The Pastor Is in a Bad Place

CHAPTER ONE

Burned Out (Or Something Like It)

You probably know the metaphor about boiling a frog. Supposedly, if you drop a frog into a pot of boiling water, the sudden heat will spur it to action. The frog will immediately jump out of the pot, saving its life in the process. If you put a frog in cool water, though, and slowly raise the temperature up to the boiling point, the frog won't realize what's happening. It will just stay in that pot of water while the ever-increasing temperature eventually cooks it to death.

I'm not sure how true this is. (Would a frog really sit still that long?) It does, though, remind me of something I experienced in my own life before I decided to take three months of renewal leave from my role as a pastor. I was the proverbial frog in the pot. Slowly and without noticing it, my prayer life, my attention to sabbath, and my enthusiasm for ministry had all slowly boiled away. I wasn't just tired, I was exhausted, and the temperature wasn't dropping. I needed to do something before my spiritual systems started shutting down.

At the time, I had been a pastor for fifteen years. When I graduated from seminary, I was fresh and full of energy. I was passionate for the work I did, even if I was a little raw and naïve. I also maintained strong boundaries between sabbath, family time, prayer, and work.

A decade and a half later, I still loved ministry. If you asked me if I could imagine doing anything else with my life, the answer would be a confident "Definitely not!" But the weight of those fifteen years, along with the gradual erosion of the boundaries I had placed around my time and my priorities, had begun to take their toll.

I've never liked when other pastors I know post those articles with titles like, "Ten Things Your Pastor Wishes You Knew About How Hard Ministry Is." In my mind, it always comes across as a little self-serving. It feels like begging for a compliment. It is true, though, that there are some aspects of being a pastor that can get to you after a while. The responsibility of providing spiritual care for a community, no matter the size, is a heavy weight to bear. There are always more tasks that need to be done around a church than there are people willing to do them. Plus, the proximity of many parsonages to the church makes it really easy to say, "I'll just go over and do something quick at the church," only to stay far longer than originally anticipated. Those hours build up over time.

There are other things too that may seem positive at first, but ultimately turn into something sour. For instance, church members can be sooooo appreciative when you do something nice or thoughtful for them! It makes you want to do the same for someone else, then for someone else, and then for someone else after that. Before you realize it, your own motivations have more to do with the desire for appreciation and pats on the back than they do with whether or not the things you're doing actually need to be done, or, more importantly, whether they need to be done by you.

Simply put, the job of a modern pastor is complex. A 2019 study published by the Alban Institute identified sixty-four different competencies clergy needed in order to do their work well. *Sixty-four different skills!*[1] In a single day, a clergyperson might be called on to pray with a patient in the hospital, brainstorm a solution to a facilities maintenance issue, lead a Bible study, comfort a grieving family, write a sermon, and craft a stewardship campaign. Can you do sixty-four different things extremely well? No? Don't worry, neither can anyone else. Too often though, our own expectation—and the expectation of the churches we serve—is that we will be able to take on all these tasks and execute them appropriately. When that proves impossible, we start to fall behind. We get frustrated, our church members get frustrated, and ultimately we either over-work ourselves to try to make up for what we see as our failings or shut down completely. It's the perfect recipe for burnout.

Recognizing the Signs

Looking back, I'd known for a while that something needed to change. More nights than not, I'd come home, collapse on the couch, and announce to my wife, "I'm exhausted." I didn't just mean I was tired after a long day at work; I was feeling a deep soul-level exhaustion. I began to notice that it was harder to come up with sermon ideas, harder to find something new to say in those sermons, and harder to start on the next sermon after I'd just finished preaching the last one. Sometimes these are signs that a pastor needs to move to a new church, but I truly felt like there was still a lot of fruitful ministry to be done at the church where I was serving. I was simply having more and more trouble summoning the passion to do it.

---

1. Matt Bloom, *Flourishing In Ministry: How to Cultivate Clergy Wellbeing* (Lanham, MD: Rowman & Littlefield, 2019), p. 9.

In her book, *Strengthening the Soul of Your Leadership*, Ruth Haley Barton lists several warning signs that indicate a spiritual leader is seriously depleted and "may be functioning beyond human limitations."[2] Discussing her list, Barton writes, "If even a few of these symptoms are true for you, chances are you are pushing up against human limitations and you, too, might need to consider that 'what you are doing is not good' for you or for the people you are serving."[3] When I read her checklist, more than half applied to me.

Two warning signs in particular described me well in the months leading up to my renewal leave. The first was that I was hoarding energy, or taking steps to protect myself from certain interactions with other people because I knew the situation would drain the last of my energy reserves. I'm a naturally curious person, so when someone comes into the church building, I tend to wander out into the hallway to see who it is and find out what's been going on in their life. As I pondered Barton's description of this warning sign, I realized that lately I'd been staying in my office more often when someone came into the church, instead of going out to greet them. It was just easier and less tiring.

The other warning sign I recognized in myself was a failure to realize that spiritual practices like prayer and journaling had ceased to be life-giving. Instead, they'd become yet another task that consumed time and energy. Maintaining a routine of regular, daily prayer has been a challenge throughout my ministry, particularly during the church's busiest seasons. In the past, when I did take time to pray during those busiest times, it came as a relief. It felt like sitting down

2. Barton, Ruth Haley, *Strengthening the Soul of Your Leadership: Seeking God in the Crucible of Ministry*, 2nd edition (Downers Grove, IL: IVP Books, 2018), p. 104.
3. Ibid, p. 106

with my best friend for some much-needed quality time after several days of waving at each other in passing. In the months before
I took renewal leave, something fundamental changed in the way I
approached prayer. I wasn't necessarily praying less, but prayer had
lost its sense of joy for me. I was losing the sense of prayer as a life-
giving conversation with my Creator and beginning to treat it as
more of a task to check off my list before getting around to writing
sermons and visiting parishioners.

As I reflected on these things, I realized that, in addition to my
role as lead pastor, I had also unintentionally drifted into acting as
one of the youth group leaders at the church I was serving. This is
when I *should* have known that I needed to do something different.
After losing our previous youth leader, my wife Julie and I offered to
lead the group for a few months until someone new could be hired.
In many ways, this made sense. One of our children was in the youth
group, and I'd had a lot of the other youth in my confirmation classes.
I wanted to make sure they didn't miss out on spiritual growth during
the transition.

Those months leading the youth group were great. We deepened
our relationships with the teens in the church. We introduced games
from our own church camp and youth group days, which translated
surprisingly well to a new generation. While our own teenager grum-
bled about his parents' constant presence at youth activities, we felt
truly blessed to be part of his spiritual growth in that way, as well as
that of his friends from church.

The problem was that a couple of months turned into six, which
then turned into a year. All that time, I was also keeping up with all
the responsibilities included in my role as lead pastor. This should
have been an obvious sign that something was seriously wrong with
my boundaries! To be clear, the church was not to blame for this

situation. I had offered to double as the leader of the youth group. I had voluntarily over-extended myself. During that year, I never voiced any major dissatisfaction with the arrangement beyond periodic reminders that they ought to be looking for a new youth leader. From their perspective, the work was being done. If the arrangement wasn't working, I was the one who needed to establish that boundary and change the situation. Instead, I kept telling them about how well things were going with the youth group under Julie's and my leadership.

To understand how I finally recognized that something needed to change, you need to know something about me: I have always prided myself on giving 100 percent in ministry. I may not be the best preacher you'll ever hear, but I work hard on every sermon. I may not always have the most eloquent words during a pastoral visit, but I try to be fully present for each person I am visiting. I have done my best throughout my ministry to apply the same standard to everything I do at the churches I serve. That's how I could tell something was wrong when I had a few significant ministry moments where I knew my heart wasn't completely in it. I hadn't given my best, and it bothered me.

No one ever said anything. No one said they were dissatisfied with the ministry I had provided. In fact, I got positive feedback from one of them. After fifteen years of ministry, it turned out that I could give less than 100 percent and still do well enough. As far as I know, I was the only person who noticed that I wasn't giving my all. But I did notice, and it scared me. It made me wonder if I was starting to become someone I never, ever wanted to be.

I had seen them around at conferences and other events. You've seen them too. You might even know a few personally. They're the burned-out pastors who sit around tables with other clergy complaining about their congregations. These are the pastors—our colleagues—who are just trying to get to retirement, just trying to get to the point where they can trade a paycheck for a Social Security check. These are the pastors who have been giving less than 100 percent for so long that they don't even realize they're phoning it in anymore. Guess what? They didn't get there overnight.

My wife Julie says I live and die by the snowball effect. She says that I always assume a single event that's only a little bit bad will eventually pick up steam and spiral into something truly awful. When a single sermon doesn't quite connect with the congregation, that just may be the beginning of a permanent slide into preaching mediocrity. When one worship service doesn't go quite as I planned, it could lead to people leaving the church. While my concerns about my passion for ministry could have just been another example of this tendency, this seemed somehow different. When I found myself giving less than my best in moments that were important to others—and should have been equally important to me—I saw a possible future ahead of me that I didn't like one bit. Once I realized this, I started talking to people about it.

Taking the First Steps

First, I talked to Julie, who has been my spouse for a year longer than I've been a pastor. Julie knows my ministry better than anyone else, and in many ways, she knows me better than I know myself. She is the person whose opinion I trust more than anyone in the world. It wasn't an easy conversation to start, but I'm glad I did. When I told her I thought something wasn't quite right in my ministry and spiritual life, Julie responded, "I've known for a while that there was something wrong. I'm glad you've finally realized it." It turned out that my physical and spiritual exhaustion had been affecting our whole family, and I was the last to notice. Julie shared with me that recently I'd been less focused when I was home, less engaged with family activities, and less capable of dealing with adversity when it came up. I thought I was handling my exhaustion well, but the truth was that everybody else who lived in our house had noticed.

This was the first of several conversations Julie and I had over the course of a few weeks. Eventually, we decided that I should talk to my supervisor in ministry. In my denomination, that person is called a district superintendent. In my case, that was Mitch.

I spent a lot of time talking to Mitch. He was patient with me as I talked things through. My thoughts were scattered and confused. I knew why I was there, but I didn't know exactly what I was asking or what could be done. I just knew that I was tired and something needed to change. Mitch asked me whether I thought it was time to move to a new congregation, but I told him no, there was still ministry for me to do at the church where I was serving. Finally, he said the words that made all the difference in my ministry: "I wonder if you should take renewal leave."

Every clergyperson in my denomination is eligible for renewal leave, but, until recently, very few took advantage of it. Even when a pastor did take renewal leave, they were often on their way either into or out of a position within the church hierarchy. Most pastors serving in local churches wouldn't even have considered taking several months away from their congregation. How would the church continue to function? Who would preach? Who would make decisions? And the most concerning question: What happens if the congregation realizes they actually can get by for months at a time without all the things a pastor does to manage the congregation's life together? It's a scary proposition.

However, while taking a step away from ministry might be scary, it can also be healthy. The practices and policies of my denomination establish renewal leave as a foundational element in the rhythm of a pastoral life. The practice of renewal leave is rooted in the biblical concept of a Sabbath year. In Leviticus 25:4-5, the Israelites are commanded to let the land rest once every seven years. The people are told that, for this year, "You shall not sow your field or prune your vineyard. You shall not reap the aftergrowth of your harvest or gather the grapes of your unpruned vine: it shall be a year of complete rest for the land," (Lev. 25:4b-5). Significantly, this also provided rest for those who cared for the land.

There are a variety of programs designed specifically to help pastors looking to take renewal leave, and some of them are very generous with the grant money they offer. I knew pastors who had received major grants that allowed them to spend their time doing astounding things like horseback riding for a month in Ireland or taking sailing lessons on the Mediterranean Sea off the coast of Greece. I like horses! Greece sounds nice!

While I debated applying for a grant like this, I ultimately decided against it. If I got a grant, there would have been almost two years between when I realized I needed renewal leave and when I would actually start my time away from the church. That translated into hundreds of pastoral visits and countless other administrative tasks before I took my renewal leave, as well as ninety-six more sermons until I got the break I knew I needed. Truthfully, I'm not sure which was more disconcerting—the number of sermons, or the fact I knew what the number was! More sobering was the realization that if I didn't get a big grant the first time around, I'd have to wait even longer.

At the end of the day, the most significant reason I chose not to apply for the grant was also the simplest: I just didn't feel like I needed a big, pull-out-all-the-stops international trip to restore my soul. What I really wanted—what I craved—was time and space to catch up on the things I'd been missing over the past fifteen years of ministry. I needed solitude and silence to connect with my Creator on a deep and intimate level. I needed the opportunity to sit with my family in a pew during a worship service. I needed the freedom to jump in the car and drive somewhere for a whole weekend without needing to be back by Sunday morning. I needed to free my brain from the constant strain of writing sermons and long-term planning. I needed the time to dig deep into the theological reading I loved back when I was in seminary. I was confident that I could accomplish all these things on a reasonable budget.

A Reclamation Project

When I was in high school, a man named Dr. Keith Roberts was my Sunday school teacher. He was a sociology professor at a nearby college and much of his work focused on the sociology of religion. Later in his life, years after I was in his Sunday school class, Dr. Roberts wrote a book based on his experience living with a stage IV cancer diagnosis. Rather than using the well-known metaphors of battle and war, he chose to write about it in the terms of a "reclamation project." The imagery he used was taken from his own experience watching a polluted community dumping ground in St. Paul, Minnesota, restored to its original wetland condition by the Dakota people who lived around it:

It had been a wetland ravine—a place of birthing and beginnings for the Dakota—but all the water had been drained, and it had become a dump fouled with pollutants and filled with refrigerators and other appliances that residents had tossed there. In recent years, and with the help of some federal funds, the Dakota and others have been cleaning up this site. The trashed appliances have been removed, the water levels are coming back, and strategic native plants that either absorb chemicals or provide nutrients and renew the soil have been planted.[4]

This image of a reclamation project spoke to my soul. While my situation was obviously far less dire than that of Dr. Roberts, I was also in need of restoration and renewal. As I began to plan my renewal leave, I envisioned it as my own personal "reclamation project," a mission to reclaim my passion and my energy for the ministry to which God had called me to dedicate my life.

With this defining metaphor in mind, I identified several goals for my renewal leave on a budget. First, I wanted to spend time with my family. Three months without evening meetings, without weddings and funerals on the weekends, and without the pressure of weekly sermon preparation meant more time for my immediate family, as well as trips to visit our family that lived further away.

Second, I wanted to restore my spiritual life. I wanted to reconnect with God and relearn the spiritual discipline of deep and meaningful prayer. I wanted to reawaken the part of my intellect that was nourished by serious theological thought. I wanted to engage with

4. Roberts, Keith A., *Meaning-Making With Malignancy: A Theologically Trained Sociologist Reflects On Living Meaningfully with Cancer.* Murrells Inlet, SC (2018), Covenant Books.

the work of great Christian thinkers, both current and historical. To achieve this, I would need to find some quiet, empty spaces and some time alone to reflect and pray.

Finally, I wanted to take stock of my work in ministry. After fifteen years, I figured I was roughly at the midpoint of my career. I wanted time to look back on the last decade and a half and to begin looking forward to what was ahead.

Everything was finally decided. I'd had conversations about renewal leave with my wife and with my denominational and congregational leadership. I'd determined how I would fund my renewal leave. I had identified a defining metaphor to frame the time I spent away from my congregation, and I'd developed goals for this time of rest and reclamation. Now it was time to start spreading the news and putting my plans into action.

† † †
Is Your Spark Burning Out?

Take a piece of paper and write "Burnout Early Warning Signs" at the top of the page. Then, make two columns on the paper with the center line running about two-thirds of the way down the page. Title one column "How I Feel" and the other "Things I've Noticed." In the first column, write down anything you sense within you that suggests you might be headed toward burnout. Are you having trouble sleeping at night? How's your prayer life? These are the sorts of things you're looking for. In the other column, note any situations you've noticed in your ministry or in your life that you think might indicate a lack of boundaries, a lack of self-care, or a lack of passion that could be related to burnout. For me, I had developed a reticence to come out of my office and talk to people I heard coming into the church.[5]

Once you've completed these two lists, put the paper aside for twenty-four hours. On the following day, pick it back up and review it. As you read the items you've written on your lists, ask yourself, "If I saw these signs in a pastoral colleague, what feedback would I give them?"

---

5. If either of these lists include any thoughts of self-harm or other serious physical, mental, or emotional symptoms, contact your physician or a mental health provider immediately.

CHAPTER TWO

The Road to Renewal

One of my wife's favorite people is someone she has never met in person. Every few months, I spend an incredibly valuable hour talking with Janet, a counselor with a practice near our church. Since she doesn't have any connection to my congregation, I can talk with her about all things going on at the church and get her unbiased opinion. As a leader in her own church, she understands the challenges of ministry and can relate to many of the issues I'm facing. Most importantly, Janet has no problem telling me that I need to turn my struggles over to the Lord, who can handle it far better than I can. Julie says Janet is one of her favorite people because I always come back from these conversations calmer, more focused, and mentally well-balanced.

When I brought up the idea of renewal leave, and that I was considering whether or not to apply for it, Janet excitedly responded, "Wait! You mean that's even a possibility? Why didn't you ever bring this up before? You've needed this for a while."

I acknowledged that she was probably right and added that I thought it might be good for me. She, however, was not going to passively accept this equivocating and told me straight out, "You *think* it might be good for you? Come on, Greg. You *know* it would be good for you."

I laughed apprehensively and told her that, yes, I did know it, but I also didn't want to get my hopes up. I was worried about what would happen if it wasn't approved or if the church had reservations. Thankfully, Janet continued to push me and wouldn't let my fears get in the way of what I needed. She boldly proclaimed, "I'll tell you exactly what you're going to do if that happens. You are going to come right back into my office, and we're going to figure out how you're going to get three months away from being a pastor!"

So, yeah, you could say my counselor was on board with the idea.

Working Through Concerns

That was one important conversation on my journey to renewal leave. Even more important was the ongoing conversation I was having with my wife. In the months before I applied for renewal leave, I wavered back and forth on whether I was going to go through with this at all. I had a running list in my mind of all the reasons why it was potentially a bad idea. It was going to be so much work to get ready to be away from the church for three months. I would have to wrap up projects I was working on, train others to take over tasks I was responsible for, find someone to preach ... and that was just the beginning of the list. Additionally, the church leadership might not go for it. What if I got bored after only a few weeks? What would happen then? The excuses went on and on.

These concerns were minor compared to the two more substantial reasons I considered not taking renewal leave, both of which demanded careful thought and prayer. The first was the burden it would place on my family. Julie and I are what's known as a "clergy couple." I am the pastor of a church and Julie is a chaplain. Both of us are in highly demanding, intense roles. Both of us could have used some time away from the rigors of ministry. While I would be on renewal leave, though, Julie would not. Because of this, our opportunities to be away from home together would be limited by her work schedule. This meant that I would often be traveling by myself, and I wasn't sure how I felt about having exciting new adventures without being able to share them with my wife.

Beyond that, Julie and I are blessed to be the parents of two wonderful boys, who were seven and thirteen at the time I was considering taking leave. During the parts of my renewal leave when I'd be traveling without the rest of the family, Julie would be solely responsible for getting them to school and after-school activities. All the cooking, the cleaning, and the other household chores that we usually divide up between us would fall on her shoulders. And remember, she would be doing all this while also continuing in her ministry as a chaplain. While many single parents manage to successfully balance this lifestyle, it's hard work, and it had not been our pattern for the sixteen years we'd been married. I felt like it would be a betrayal to our marriage—and to the expectations we had developed together over the course of our marriage—to be away for several weeks over the course of the summer, particularly when Julie didn't have the same opportunity.

The second substantial reason I considered not applying for renewal leave was my concern about what I might learn about myself and my call to ministry. For fifteen years, I had been doing pastoral ministry nonstop. It was all I could do to keep up with the demands of church and family life, and there had never really been time to slow down. There had never been time to pause and take stock of my ministry. Fifteen years is a long time. I knew that many things about me, personally, had changed. What would happen if my call had changed, too, and I finally slowed down long enough to notice?

This was not merely a philosophical concern, but a deeply practical one. I have an undergraduate degree in history and a master's degree in divinity. Aside from summer jobs in college, nearly all the paid work I've done in my adult life has been church-related. I was a missionary teacher for a year, a missionary carpenter for a year, a seminary resident housing manager for a year, and a theology professor's research assistant for a year. Then I became a pastor, and I've been holding that same role in one church or another ever since. Other than being a minister, I am qualified to do ... basically nothing. If I realized that I wasn't called to be a pastor anymore, our family would be out one parsonage and one paycheck.

Thankfully, Julie refused to let me use either of these concerns as reasons not to take renewal leave. She would patiently listen as I talked through my concerns, and then she would reassure me, saying, "I hear your apprehension, but from my perspective none of those seem like reasons you shouldn't take renewal leave. Here's why I think you should." Julie's list of reasons why I *should* take renewal leave was every bit as long as my list of reasons why I *shouldn't*. Even though it would be hard juggling everything while I was away, she said that my renewal leave would still end up being good for all of us. Julie reminded me that I was struggling and that this was already affecting us as a couple and as a family. As for what would happen if I realized I wasn't called to be a pastor anymore? Well, we'd figure something out. There were other houses in the world if we couldn't live in a parsonage. If I had to be in transitionary phase while I figured out what kind of work a former pastor is qualified to do, we still had Julie's income and our savings to draw from. She didn't tell me that my fears were groundless; instead she helped me see them as obstacles that could be overcome.

Did I tell you my wife is amazing?

Hard Conversations

Being married to someone whom I can have hard conversations with is one of the great blessings of my life. It would have been far easier for Julie—at least in the short term—to say, "You know, I think you're right. We're not at a place in our life right now where we can accommodate you taking three months off to pray and travel and explore your call." Instead, she realized before I did that if I continued along the path I was on—if I didn't do something to change my trajectory—the long-term effects would far outweigh the short-term hardships created by a three-month renewal leave. Without being unkind or trying to force me into anything I genuinely didn't want to do, she created space for me to reconnect with my call and restore my soul by taking renewal leave.

If you are considering renewal leave, it is vital that you have the two conversations I've described in this chapter before you have any others. If you are married, it is essential that your spouse be in agreement that this is a good idea. It simply would not have been possible to have a successful renewal leave without my spouse's support. Not only did we have to dig into the proverbial couch cushions of our bank accounts and reallocate money that could have been used elsewhere to pay for my travels, the times I was traveling on my own also put a significant burden on Julie. I went through some pretty deep spiritual and emotional soul-searching during those three months, and being the chief listener through all of it put a heavy weight on her at times. Renewal leave was good for all of us in the long run, but it was not easy, and it did not come without cost.

As described at the beginning of this chapter, I also think it's important to find someone to talk to *other* than your spouse. This person should have a good sense of where you are mentally and emotionally. Renewal leave is a great solution to a very specific problem, but there are all sorts of other, deeper things that could be going on in your life for which renewal leave isn't the right answer. What if that sense of tiredness and lethargy is actually clinical depression? Could that activity you're spending more and more time on have become a kind of addiction that's not leaving room for anything else in your life, including ministry? Is your sense of dissatisfaction and restlessness an indication that you need to work on damaged relationships, or could it be the Holy Spirit telling you it's time to move to a different church?

Janet, my counselor, was the right person for me to talk to about this. Personally, I think every pastor should have a counselor they talk to from time to time, but if you don't, perhaps a clergy colleague who knows you well—maybe someone you're in a covenant group or have a significant relationship with—can help fill this role of trusted advisor. It needs to be someone who can listen without judgment when you tell them you're feeling less passion for ministry than you once did. It must be someone who will hold your conversations in confidence. And it should be someone who is wise enough that they'll have helpful things to say. Whoever it is, they ought to be someone who can retain some level of objectivity as they listen to you and can give you honest feedback.

Telling the Leadership

Finally, after working through these two crucial conversations, I was ready to approach the lay leadership of the church with my plan. At the time, I had been the pastor of Main Street United Methodist Church for five years. During this time, I had developed close pastoral relationships and a built up a high level of trust with the leadership of the church. We'd made hard decisions together and worked on long-range plans. I had prayed with them during personal challenges, when they were in the hospital, and at the gravesides of their family members. We had broken bread together at the Communion table and at church dinners. I was not worried at all that they would think less of me, as a person or as a pastor, when I told them I was thinking about taking renewal leave because I was mentally, spiritually, and emotionally exhausted.

I was, however, less certain about their response to the idea itself. While it has become more common in recent years for pastors to take renewal leave, Main Street had never had a pastor go through this process before. It's a small church with no associate pastor to take over preaching and pastoral care responsibilities. Additionally, since the parsonage is on the same property as the church, I would literally be living in their backyard for three months but not preparing sermons, visiting people, or coming in to the office.

It turned out that I didn't need to be worried. When I brought up the idea to the core leaders of the church, their responses ranged from "I absolutely agree that you need to do this" to "If this is what you need to do, we'll figure it out." One of my priorities at Main Street has been to develop strong lay leadership and empower the leaders of the congregation to take responsibility for their church. Therefore, it was gratifying—not to mention humbling—to hear one of the key administrative leaders say she couldn't wait until I started my renewal leave! She explained, "It feels like you've been preparing us for this for the past five years. Now we get to take a test run and see how it goes."[1]

Once I'd talked to the lay leadership, we immediately formed two teams. The first was a Renewal Leave Team, which would be responsible for developing a cohesive plan for the three months that I would be away. This group would be the point of contact for any concerns that arose from the congregation, either before or during the renewal leave. They would also determine when, if ever, to contact me and ask me to temporarily resume my duties before my renewal leave had come to an end.

The second team I referred to as my Intervention Team. This group consisted of one of the lay leaders of the church, the church office manager, and Julie. These were the three people who observed my ministry the closest and who worked most directly with me on most ministry projects. I asked them to help me identify things I was doing that made my ministry more difficult than necessary, as well as things I could eliminate from my workload that would free me up for more essential ministry tasks both now and once I returned from renewal leave. Julie and the church lay leader, who both have training as social workers, quickly agreed. The office manager went a step farther and told me, "I've been waiting for you to ask, because I've got a list!"

---

1. If you do face resistance, it's important to not panic or get defensive, but it's also important to stay firm in what you know to be true. You know you need renewal leave. You've prayed about it and sought the advise of wise and trusted friends and colleagues. If you have support from denominational leadership or other leaders beyond the local church, consider going back to them and asking for help making the case for renewal leave.

Both teams were essential parts of my renewal leave. The Renewal Leave Team worked hard to work out every detail so the summer would go smoothly. They asked a lot of questions that began with, "What will we do if . . ." or "How will we handle [fill in the blank] while Greg's away?" The Intervention Team helped me begin to address the root causes that led me to need renewal leave in the first place. These two teams deserve a lot of credit for making my renewal leave a success that continues to bear fruit even now, years later.

Telling the Congregation

When the announcement was made to the congregation, the feedback was largely positive. There were a few people who didn't think it was right for a pastor to take three months off, and, honestly, I couldn't blame them—there was part of me that felt the same way. However, there were others who had seen the signs before I did, even if they couldn't quite put a name to them. Early in my renewal leave, I ran into a parishioner one day when I was out getting a haircut. She shared with me, "After you told us you were going to take time away, I started watching you closely. I could tell how much you needed it, and I'm glad you're taking it."

Of course, church members did have questions and concerns about what would happen during my renewal leave. There were three specific concerns that came up repeatedly. The first was about who would fill the pulpit while I was away. In the early stages of planning, we had considered the possibility of having people from the congregation take turns preaching. We ultimately decided against this option, as it seemed likely to make the three months feel disjointed to the congregation. Instead, we decided to ask a retired pastor named Steve to fill the pulpit every Sunday for the entire three months. It was a great choice. Steve was dynamic, funny, and laid back. He made an immediate connection with the congregation that deepened over the three months he preached in my place.[2]

The second concern voiced by church members was financial. The church's finance chair received several questions about the nature of paid renewal leave for pastors in my denomination. Was it right, the questioners asked, for a church to have to pay two pastors? This was a very legitimate question, at least in my opinion, and it was one that Julie and I had asked ourselves earlier in the process. In response to this concern, we decided to donate to the church an amount that was equal to most of Steve's stipend for the three months I was away. While some of the clergy colleagues I talked to disagreed with this decision, we felt like it was the right thing to do based on our context and our financial ability to do so. As it turned out, the congregation felt like it was the right thing, as well. The finance chair shared with me that almost everyone from the congregation who questioned the financial burden on the church had their concerns alleviated when they heard that the Pimlotts would be personally donating most of the stipend for pulpit supply.

The final concern was more personal and was most poignantly voiced by a parishioner who had been in poor health on-and-off for years. One day, before my renewal leave began, she stopped me in the

2. Years before, Steve answered a call from God to plant a church in a cornfield in a rural area about an hour away from our church. That cornfield church plant quickly became a huge congregation that is still vibrant today. Now, in their retirement, Steve and his wife Barbara split their time between a trailer in Florida and a house a few miles away from our church. While Steve was quite content to stay retired, the opportunity to spend a few months back in the pulpit appealed to him. I will be forever grateful to Steve for stepping in to help me out and filling the pulpit in my stead.

hallway of the church and told me, "You know, Greg, I'm glad you have the opportunity to do this. It's just that I'm ninety-two years old . . ." Immediately, my eyes filled with tears because I knew exactly what she meant, and how important it was.

This was the biggest church-related concern I had as I was considering renewal leave. The role of the pastor is a sacred one. We are privileged to walk with our parishioners through the highs and lows of their lives. They often tell us things they haven't even told some of their closest family members. When they die, we are there consoling their family and proclaiming the good news of Jesus Christ, who conquered death through his resurrection.

When I talked to my church leadership about situations that would cause me to temporarily come back from renewal leave, they told me firmly, "If you're not going to come back for the funeral of everyone's distant cousin who dies, we don't want you to come back for anyone." After some negotiation, and at my insistence, they agreed to at least call me back from my renewal leave if a child or teen in the congregation were to become critically ill or die. Additionally, they agreed to call me back if there was a catastrophic disaster in our community with multiple fatalities or massive property loss. Still, it was no easy thing to hear the Renewal Leave Team tell the congregation, "Greg will be on leave for three months, and we will not be asking him to come back—even for funerals."

Thank goodness the church had Betty, the lay volunteer in charge of our congregational care team. Betty is a retired hospital social worker who has spent countless hours in her retirement volunteering at the church. During my renewal leave, a beloved member of the church named Grace died. Since Betty had visited Grace several times in the hospital and had prayed with Grace and her family as she drew her last breaths, Betty was asked to lead her funeral. A few days later, Betty led the congregation and community in expressing their collective grief at Grace's death and their hope in resurrection through Jesus Christ.

When I returned from renewal leave, Betty said to me, "It was a wonderful experience, and I'm so glad I was able to do that for Grace. And I sure am glad you're back!" The church's willingness to care for the dead and grieving in my absence was one of the greatest gifts the congregation gave me in connection with my renewal leave.

After several intense but important conversations and months of planning, the start date of my renewal leave was drawing near. I was feeling more and more comfortable about the idea of stepping away for three months. With the Renewal Leave Team in place, a pastor ready to provide support in my absence, and a full three months of rest, travel, prayer, and spiritual reading on my calendar, I was ready to see what God had in store for me. With the Holy Spirit as my guide, I was ready to spend the next three months on my renewal leave reclamation project.

CHAPTER THREE

I Can't Do This!

"This was a bad idea," I said. "I don't think I can really do this!"

It was only the second day of my renewal leave and I was standing in the road talking to one of my church's lay leaders. I had flagged down her down as she was driving out of the parking lot after a church meeting that had just ended. How did I know it had just ended? Well, I'd been watching the parking lot from our living room window waiting for people to come out of the building so I could find out what happened.

This wasn't a particularly important gathering of church leadership. In fact, it was pretty routine. No big decisions were being made, no major votes were taken, and nothing special was on the agenda. It was, however, the first meeting to take place since I'd gone on renewal leave the day before, and the not-knowing was killing me. As they met, I sat in the parsonage obsessing. I felt guilty that I wasn't there as their pastor. I worried that they might have a question that only I could answer. What if they needed me and I wasn't around?

They didn't need me. They were fine.

About six months before the start of my renewal leave, I mounted a big dry-erase board on my office wall and listed all the projects I was leading or involved in at the church. Under each project, I wrote all the tasks I needed to complete before I left for three months. When I closed my office door for the last time, I wanted to be completely caught up on all those projects. I didn't want to leave unfinished work for other people to complete, and I needed a visual way to gauge how close I was to accomplishing that goal. If I succeeded, the white board would be empty by the time my renewal leave started.

It came down to the wire, but I got it done. I finished every task. It took a lot of extra hours on evenings, weekends, and early mornings to clear that dry-erase board, but on the day before I left I erased the last item on the list and stepped away from pastoral ministry as completely caught up as it is possible for a pastor to be.

Knowing this, an inquisitive observer might ask why I kept finding reasons to wander over to the church during the first week of my renewal leave. They might wonder why I kept gazing longingly at the parking lot every time there were cars present. The answer is that I couldn't help myself! I was curious and kept wondering what was going on at the church that I might be missing.

On the second morning of my renewal leave, Julie was at work and the kids were completing their morning routine of chores, reading, and playing outside. Nobody at home needed me right then, and it occurred to me that I was not particularly happy about it! Here's what I wrote in my journal:

> Day Two of renewal leave, and, to be honest, I am not having much fun. Yesterday was a very nice day of relaxing, and staying in bed reading, playing games with the boys, and doing some satisfying and gratifying deep cleaning of the kitchen.

But this morning, I'm feeling restless and grumpy. Everyone else's life is going on, and I'm the only one out of rhythm. . . .

At the church, they're gearing up for the first Sunday of worship while I'm on renewal leave, but there's nothing on my dry-erase board of things I need to do, and the key to my office is on the office manager's desk in an envelope marked "For Steve."

In short, this stinks.

Bear in mind that this was only the *second* day of my renewal leave! If my entire renewal leave continued like this, it was going to be a miserable three months.

While it may sound obvious, I was learning that just because I was on renewal leave, that didn't mean everyone else was, too. The boys had their daily summer routines. Julie was at work. Most of my non-church-member friends in the area were pastors who certainly didn't have time for me to come hang out at their offices all day to chat! Like many pastors, I'm a highly relational person, yet I had all this time on my hands and nobody to share it with.

I also came to realize that there was a deeper problem. I had completely lost the ability to not do something at all times. I had lost the ability to rest. As I reflected further, I realized that my vacations and Sabbath days had taken on a disturbingly predictable pattern. I would rest for a little bit—perhaps one full day on vacation, or a couple of hours on my Sabbath day each week—but I couldn't resist filling the rest of the time with tasks and activities. If we were at home, I'd clean out the garage, balance the checkbook, cook—anything to keep me busy. If we were traveling, I'd mark up the pages of guidebooks and try to pack as many activities as possible into the limited time we had together.

I'd always prided myself on hustling harder than the next person. Over time, this had become a fundamental part of my identity. Then, suddenly, I was confronted with three months—*ninety full days*— where the entire idea was to not hustle, not fill up a dry-erase board, and not fill every open spot on my calendar. Instead, I was supposed to rest, leave the board empty, and wait for God to make the agenda. It turned out that I was bad at that.

It became increasingly clear that I needed more than just a few months' rest; I needed to revise my entire understanding of pastoral ministry. Somewhere along the way, I'd fallen prey to the idea that the success of churches I served—which are the visible representation of Jesus in their communities, ordained and empowered by the Holy Spirit—depended on *my* hard work as a pastor rather than our shared obedience to God. Not only was that an assumption that bordered on blasphemy, it was also an impossible expectation to live up to, and one that I had imposed on myself.

I needed to learn how to define myself as something other than the tasks that I accomplished, something more than by my role as an ordained minister. I needed to learn how to view myself as a child of God, under God's care and direction. I needed to acknowledge that I had unwittingly become like Martha in Luke's Gospel. I had become distracted by my tasks while Jesus himself was waiting for me to come and sit with him. While I was frantically completing everything on my to-do list, I was missing the chance to sit at his feet, to rest, and to grow in his love and grace. I needed to open my ears to hear Jesus speak to me, as he did to Martha so long ago, "You are worried and distracted by many things, but few things are needed—indeed only one." (Luke 10:41-42a). I just wasn't sure I still knew how to respond to that invitation once I heard it.

This resting was clearly going to be hard work.

Stepping Back

Stepping back from my pastoral duties was significantly harder than I thought it would be! The first week of renewal leave was challenging, to say the least. It also helped me identify some issues about myself and my identity as a pastor—like a need to be needed and an inability to rest—that led me to need renewal leave in the first place.

How hard do you think it would be for you to step away from your regular pastoral responsibilities for several weeks or months? What specific challenges would you face? Take out a piece of paper and make a list of your main responsibilities in your current role. Next, make a separate list of the challenges you would face in stepping away from those responsibilities for a time. Be specific! (And be honest!)

When you're finished, look at the list of challenges. What does this list tell you about yourself as a pastor? If you saw this list from an outsider's perspective, what observations would you make?

† † †
PART TWO

The Pastor Makes a Decision

CHAPTER FOUR

How Do I Know When It's Time?

The first step in planning for renewal leave is deciding whether the time is right for you to step away for a few months. This involves a lot of deep prayer and vulnerable conversations with people who know you and love you. These people are the single most important resource you will have as you try to decide whether you're ready to take renewal leave. Take a minute and write down the names of the two or three most important people that you need to talk to as you discern whether the time is right for you to take renewal leave. These should be people that you trust and people who will be honest with you, even if that honesty might sting at first.

After you've written down these names, ask yourself some of the following questions. Again, this is a time to be honest with yourself. It will be helpful in the long run!

1) Am I in a good place, generally speaking?

There are two different kinds of renewal leaves. One usually takes place after something big happens at the church. This could be a massive catastrophe that requires a pastor to use every single drop of pastoral energy to lead the congregation through a difficult season, a building project that consumes a pastor's every waking moment for a long period of time, or a major conflict between a pastor and church leadership. This first type of renewal leave is for when something is acutely wrong and a pastor needs serious and immediate care. It's like a trip to the emergency room and often happens at the end of a pastor's tenure at a church.

While that type of renewal leave is also vitally important, it's not the type of renewal leave that I'll be focusing on in this book. The kind of renewal leave I'm talking about is more like preventative care when things are going fine, but you've started to notice a few areas where you're struggling a little bit. Maybe you're dealing with excessive fatigue, having trouble staying motivated, or experiencing other early warning signs of burnout. You don't need to move to another church, but you do know that something needs to change. When you've started noticing signs like these but things haven't yet become desperate, that's the perfect time to think about taking renewal leave.

I asked Mitch, my Conference Superintendent and the person who first recommended that I consider taking time away from the church, how he identifies pastors who might be ready for the preventative-care type of renewal leave. Here's how he responded:

> I think there are cues that can be recognized by anyone who's actually paying attention. It may or may not appear outwardly as fatigue, despondence, or any of the obvious signs. Oftentimes, a pastor will verbalize, without even realizing it, a note of "trapped-ness". . . .

In your case, I think I just observed a shift in energy—maybe even a subtle contradiction or qualification of language and affect that normally exudes joy.[1]

Mitch's observation is important. There are recognizable cues pointing to a pastor's need for renewal leave. Picking up on them and acting on them can be the difference between preventative care renewal leave now or a trip to the Renewal Leave Emergency Department later.

2) Are things generally going well at my church right now?

Renewal leave inevitably involves a disruption for your congregation and its ministry. For your church to get the maximum benefit from your renewal leave, the following should be in place:

* *Strong lay leadership.*
  Find a capable, established leader who is well respected by the congregation and recruit that person to be the head of the church's Renewal Leave Team. This leader and the team they put together will be the ones to go to for any major decisions that need to be made during your renewal leave. In the months before your leave begins, work with the Renewal Leave Team to develop a plan that ensures all the tasks of ministry get done while you are away. Ask specific questions like these:

  1. "Who will do [fill in the blank]?"

---

1. Rev. Mitch Gieselman, e-mail message to author, March 30, 2020.

2. "Who will you call if [blank] happens while I am on renewal leave?"

3. "Who is responsible for making the final decision if there is a disagreement about [blank]?"

Make sure they know you trust them to make good decisions while you are away, and make sure the congregation knows it too.

- *Abundant communication ahead of time with the congregation.* Hearing that their pastor will be away for three months will produce a certain level of anxiety in your church members even if they have experience with pastoral renewal leaves. If they have never had a pastor take renewal leave, multiply that tenfold! The more information you can share about your renewal leave and the plans that are in place to continue essential ministries in your absence, the better your renewal leave will turn out. Try to make sure as much communication as possible comes from the Renewal Leave Team, rather than from you as the pastor. If you're like me, your first instinct will be to manage this yourself, but you're not going to be around for three months (or however long your renewal leave is). The congregation needs to see that the Renewal Leave Team is capable of taking charge and that you trust them to lead the church.

- *A sense of momentum in some area of congregational life.* Congregations have a sense of how things are going in their life together. If your membership feels like the church is stagnating or losing ground, they're not going to be eager to add in the additional stress of their pastor being away. If, on the other hand, there's a sense of momentum in some area of ministry that provides a feeling that things are growing and heading in an exciting direction—and if the congregation feels a sense of ownership in this growth—they'll be more capable of envisioning how the church can continue to thrive while you're away.

For us at Main Street, this area of momentum was our community missions. Several years earlier, we'd begun a new ministry with the modest goal of providing eight days of lunch and activities before the children in our town went back to school in the fall. We hoped to help feed hungry children during a time when they weren't getting school lunches. Four years later, this ministry had skyrocketed into a major community effort, providing more than 2,600 meals during the summer and partnering with eight churches and other community organizations. We were rapidly expanding our efforts to ensure that no child in our community had to go hungry, and the congregation was excited about this. Most importantly, I was barely involved in the organization or planning of this ministry, which gave the congregation confidence that the church's momentum wouldn't falter while I was away.

- *Something planned for after you return.*
Inevitably, some of the people at your church will wonder if they might never see you again. They will wonder if renewal leave might be a way to plan a move and avoid saying good-bye. Several people at my church certainly worried about that—and asked me about it! Renewal leave is a time for asking big questions, like whether God is calling you to stay

at the church you're currently serving, or even in the ministry altogether. Even if you do realize that it's time to move on, though, you will at least come back from your renewal leave and finish up your ministry at the church while you're figuring out what to do next.[2] Planning at least a few things for when you get back is a good way of reassuring your congregation that they really will see you again once your renewal leave is over.

3) Have you been at the church for an adequate amount of time before you start your renewal leave?

Even if you've been in ministry for quite a while and you're tired, your congregation has only experienced a small part of that ministry at their church. If you've only been at a congregation for a year or two (or maybe even three), that may not be long enough to take a renewal leave. I had been at my church for five years when I began my renewal leave. I'm not sure that even a year earlier my congregation would have been ready for me to be gone for three months.

This is particularly true if you're a lead pastor or a solo pastor. You are your congregation's spiritual and administrative guide. They look to you for guidance and direction. If you're going to be away for an extended period, it's important that you have been at the church long enough that your staff and lay leadership have a good idea what your counsel would be if a situation comes up while you're away. If your leadership team often finds themselves wondering how you would advise them in a certain situation even when you're at the church,

---

2. Unless, that is, you're planning not to. In that case, you owe it to the congregation to tell them that!

they probably don't yet have the confidence to make the best decisions while you're away.

Even if you haven't been at a church for very long, but you're starting to see the symptoms Mitch described (or others starting to see them in you), it's still important to address them. I knew a pastor who needed time away for prayer, reflection, and renewal, but didn't feel the time was right at his current church for him to take a full renewal leave. Instead, he talked to his church leadership, who arranged for him to take three weeks of leave to spend at home with his family resting and praying. They also immediately began planning a full-length renewal leave for him to take at a later time when the church would be better prepared for their pastor to be away.

4) Have you worked hard at your church?

This is an uncomfortable question, but it's an important one. When you propose taking renewal leave, you're asking your congregation and your denominational leadership to support you in taking an extended period away from your work at the church. Many of the people in your church also work hard, are tired, and would love to have time away to travel and read and rest. If you haven't been giving your best in ministry—if you've been phoning it in for a long time, or doing the minimum required on a regular basis—then your request for renewal leave will likely not be well received. On the other hand, if you've been working hard, if you've been showing up when your parishioners need their pastor, if you've worn yourself out helping the congregation be the house of worship and community of witness God is calling them to be, then your congregation will likely have noticed.[3] They'll know you need a rest. They will be excited (most of them, at least) for you to have this opportunity to reconnect with the parts of you that get ignored amidst the burden of pastoral work. They'll also know that they'll be getting back a refreshed, renewed pastor, ready for more passionate kingdom work.

5) Do you have a support network who will give you sound advice and encouragement during your renewal leave?

I literally could not have taken my renewal leave and experienced the benefits I did without a large group of people who were supporting me. Here's just a small sampling of those people:

- My wife, Julie, who listened patiently as I talked through all the wild ideas for my renewal leave and helped me identify the few that were actually good, and who kept our children fed and cared for while I was away on my own.
- My parents, who texted me to make sure I was safe on my travels, fed me when I came to visit, and let me borrow the old red tent from my childhood while I was camping in my hometown.

---

3. It's also true that there are churches that are never satisfied with their pastor no matter how hard the pastor works. Often, this is a sign of brokenness within the congregation and may be a significant part of the reason a pastor experiences burnout. If you find yourself in a situation like this, where you know you need renewal leave but are fairly confident your church will not be supportive, I would encourage you to reach out to a denominational official, your supervising pastor, or any other trusted person of authority who might be able to help you navigate this situation. Just remember that you don't have to navigate this on your own.

- Mitch, my Conference Superintendent, who realized the subtle and not-so-subtle changes he was noticing were indications of a need for renewal and was a relentless advocate for my renewal leave once I'd agreed to do it.

- My covenant group of pastors, who have been a consistent encouragement and support for the past fifteen years, and who were excited that I was taking renewal leave (even though they could all use it themselves) and graciously listened to my stories once I got back.

- The Renewal Leave Team at my church, who made a detailed and effective plan for the three months I would be away and led the congregation as well as I could have if I had been there.

As pastors, many of us move often and work alone a lot, so we don't always have that natural support network. If you don't have this kind of network in place already, start building it as you're putting your renewal leave plans in place. Reach out to a few people in the congregation who you feel you can trust and talk to. Identify a small group of people who would lead the church well while you are away. Contact a trusted friend or two and ask if they would let you talk through ideas with them. If it feels right, stay connected with them while you are away—text them pictures from your travels, or meet them for coffee or a meal partway through your renewal leave. By the time you are back from renewal leave, you may find that some of those people have become new, lifelong friends.

Once you've prayerfully asked and answered these questions, you likely have a good sense of whether it's time to take renewal leave. If you answered, "Yes," then it's time to figure out what to do with all that time away from your pastoral responsibilities.

CHAPTER FIVE

What to Do When You're Away (and What to Avoid)

C onsider this: You've been given the opportunity of a lifetime—
weeks upon weeks of completely unscheduled days. You have no
Sunday morning responsibilities, no funerals or weddings to officiate,
no early morning visits to the hospital to pray before surgery or emergency phone calls late at night. For possibly the first time in years,
there are whole pages of your calendar that are completely empty
and waiting to be filled. God has presented you with a blank canvas
and invited you to fill it with fabulous adventures, long stretches of
contemplation and prayer, and entire days of pure relaxation.

As I began to sketch out the details of what my leave would look
like, I chose to prioritize three things: family, travel, and solitude.
These same priorities may appeal to you or you may find renewal
and restoration in other activities. There is no one-size-fits-all version of renewal, and your plans should reflect your personality, your
preferences, and your specific needs. Having said that, I do believe

that there are some general principles that I was able to learn as I was planning my own leave which I think they'll be helpful to you as well.

1) Your plans should flow out of the goals you've established for your renewal leave.

While renewal leave can be a life-giving, energizing, and restorative time, it is not magic. You can most fully enjoy all the benefits that can come from this time away from your congregation if you're intentional about developing your plans. Before you start planning specific activities, you will want to develop at least a rough idea of your overall goals for the time you've been given. Ask yourself what you want to accomplish on your renewal leave. Are there aspects of your personality that you've been neglecting during your ministry? How do you need to grow as a person of faith? Answering these questions will help you develop goals that can guide you as you plan activities over the course of your renewal leave. This will enable you to return to active pastoral ministry refreshed and ready for more fruitful years leading your church.

During my own period of planning, I decided that my goals were to spend time with my family, work on my prayer life, and take stock of my ministry after the first fifteen years. Since I knew that I wanted to accomplish these goals before coming back from renewal leave, I was able to focus my planning on activities like taking one-on-one trips with each of my children, enjoying exciting family adventures that our entire family could go on together, spending time in quiet places like the deserts of New Mexico and the mountains of North Carolina, and seeking out in-depth conversations with mentors who knew both me and my ministry well. Each activity was meaningful in its own right (not to mention fun), but each one also contributed to the overall purpose of my renewal leave and the goals I wanted to accomplish.

2) Your plans should help you explore and connect with parts of your personality that are not fulfilled by pastoral ministry.

The life of a pastor is a rich and fulfilling one. I get paid to work at a church. I get free housing and the world's easiest commute. My kids get to experience the love and care of "church grandmas." Most importantly, I get the opportunity to tell people about Jesus for a living. I can't imagine anything else I'd rather do with my life. It's a great job!

However, being a pastor also means giving up a few things. I love spontaneous day trips and travel adventures, but weekly Sunday morning responsibilities and the constant on-call nature of being a pastor mean that my ability to indulge this part of my personality is somewhat limited. I love sitting in a sanctuary and hearing someone preach a good sermon, but that rarely happens since I preach every week.

As I began to think about the possibilities presented by my renewal leave, I realized that this was a time when I could explore these passions and connect with these parts of my personality by planning trips to all corners of the country and visiting friends' churches to hear them preach. Your list will be different than mine, but your renewal leave will similarly be a good opportunity to spend time doing the things that pastoral ministry just doesn't give you enough time or space to do.

3) Your plans should be fun, and you should have fun making them.

Planning renewal leave is almost as much fun as taking one, as long as the activities you're planning sound fun to you. I spent hours day-dreaming about the exciting and interesting things I could do during the time I would be away from the church. I made lists of all the different trips I could take with our boys. I researched monastery guest houses, train schedules, hotels, campgrounds, and bed and breakfasts. If something didn't sound like fun when I was planning it, I figured it probably wouldn't be fun while I was doing it, so I crossed it off the list. Naturally, since Julie was going to be coming with me on many of the trips, we made sure they sounded like fun to her, too!

You might have noticed that I didn't include any pastors' conferences, leadership seminars, or courses on how to preach a better sermon in my renewal leave plans. That's not an accident. I knew renewal leave was a tremendous gift, a block of unfettered free time to creatively and joyfully explore the world around me and within me. I also knew there would be time in the future to pursue those other things, and I didn't want to spend my renewal leave doing something I could just as easily do later.

As with any rule, there are, of course, exceptions. I know one pastor who included multiple preaching workshops in her renewal leave plans. In her case, it made sense. While this pastor is a natural story-teller, she had noticed that her preaching had become more didactic over time. As she moved further away from storytelling toward a more pedagogic style of preaching, she realized that she was feeling less joy when telling the story of the Gospel. To address this change she'd noticed in herself, she decided to attend a few workshops for preachers about storytelling during her renewal leave. These workshops spoke to a part of her that brought her joy and would help restore that sense of joy to her preaching.

4) Don't make plans that are bigger (or smaller) than your budget.

It is obviously a bad idea to plan a renewal leave that will cost more money than you have available, but you're not likely to do that. As a pastor, you have experience working with tight budgets, making the most of limited funds, and saving money where you can. You are probably not at much risk of planning beyond your means.

What is much more likely is that you will plan a renewal leave that costs *less* than what you have available in your budget. This is also not a good idea. As you're planning, remember that you've been given the extravagant gift of time away from your everyday pastoral responsibilities. This is a way for your congregation and your community to minister to you. They expect you to make full use of this time away, and then come back renewed with new ideas and energy for your ministry. You wouldn't intentionally underfund a ministry to your congregation or your community, and you shouldn't underfund this ministry either. Spend wisely, but remember to fully embrace the gift that has been given to you.

5) Make time for the people who are most important to you, but be cautious about making plans out of a sense of obligation to family and friends.

As I started telling people about my upcoming renewal leave, I quickly realized that I had many friends and family members who assumed I would spend part of my renewal leave visiting them. I had three months with no obligations. I had friends and family all over the country (and beyond). For fifteen years, *they* had been visiting *me* because it was so hard for me to get away for a weekend visit when they would be available to host. It only made sense that I would visit them in turn, right?

While catching up on visits would have been an enjoyable way to spend three months, it would not have accomplished the goals I set for my renewal leave. There had to be a mix of the two. To strike the right balance, I started my planning process by choosing a particular sort of trip that I wanted to take—a week in my hometown, some time in a monastery, a train excursion. If it worked out for me to include a visit to family or friends on the way, I would do it. If it didn't work out, I gave myself permission to not feel bad about it.

I did not include immediate family as part of this. I made sure that my time away from church responsibilities included large blocks of time to spend with my wife, my children, my parents, and my in-laws. As I look back on my experience, I consider this one of the most sacred and rewarding aspects of my renewal leave, and I will never forget or regret the time I spent with these family members over those three months.

6) Invest in a good book (or ten).

It goes without saying that you'll want to take your Bible with you on your renewal leave. Free from the pressure of crafting a sermon each week, you may find that you'll encounter Scripture in ways you haven't since you first started seminary. Don't be surprised to find that your romance with Scripture is rekindled and rejuvenated as part of your renewal leave. If your Bible is the only book you bring with you on your renewal leave, you'll be all right.

If you're like me, though, you'll want some other books too. One of the first purchases I made in preparation for my renewal leave was a whole pile of books, which ranged from just-for-fun murder mysteries to books on prayer and Christian contemplation. I also found renewal leave to be an excellent time to pick up a book by a theologian whose writings I'd always wanted to explore but never seemed to have time for.

Karl Barth has fascinated me ever since I read a section of *Church Dogmatics* in seminary. At the time, I likened reading Barth to the experience of riding one of those old-fashioned merry-go-rounds they used to have on elementary school playgrounds. You run as quickly as you can, pushing it so it spins as fast as possible, then you jump on and lean your head back. You twirl around and around, your head spinning this way and that. When you touch the ground again, you find yourself dizzy and dazed, but exhilarated, and you want to do it again. That's what reading Barth felt like to me.

I'd always wanted to read more of what Barth wrote—not just excerpts like in seminary, but one of his complete works. However, life as a pastor, husband, and dad doesn't lend itself to that kind of deep, intense theological reading, and I'd never gotten around to picking up any of his other writings. Renewal leave, with its three months of uninterrupted time for reading and reflection, seemed like a perfect opportunity to tackle one of Barth's major works. With advice from one of my former seminary professors, I chose *The Epistle to the Romans*, his in-depth commentary on Paul's letter to the church in Rome. It was written while Barth was still pastoring a church, and my former professor thought it might be more relevant to me than one of his more academic writings.

Karl Barth's commentary on Romans shattered me in the best possible way. It was like a slap across your face that brings you to your senses. Barth was writing in Switzerland during the 1920s, as the Nazis were beginning their rise to power in neighboring Germany. He listened to his German colleagues preach sermons week after week to congregations who were witnessing the rise of evil daily, yet all he heard were tame, pleasant lectures on the relatively recent biblical discipline of historical criticism. He spent the first ninety or so pages of his 500-plus-page commentary saying (in my liberally paraphrased summary), "What are you *doing?* Don't you know we stand condemned, judged by God's perfection that confronts and reveals our imperfection? All you're doing is serving as poorly trained, two-bit guides on an archaeological dig. WAKE UP!"

When I finished reading that first section of Barth's commentary, I thought back to all the sermons I'd preached over the past year or so. I realized how, taken as a whole, they lacked urgency. They were nice, informative, and hopefully interesting, but decidedly not urgent. As I came to this realization, I was convicted. I realized that I had been wasting the time God had given me in the pulpit when I could have been bringing a word that the congregation was dying to hear. We live in a time when actual Nazis are marching in our streets. The number of displaced persons around the world has reached a record high. Our schools and other cherished institutions are under attack. We live in a time that Karl Barth might well recognize. I had been wasting time in the pulpit, and I resolved not to waste any more.

I also realized something about the kinds of books I'd been reading over the past several years. Here's what I wrote in my journal at the time:

> I think about how much time I have spent in the past eighteen months or so reading church leadership books. They are the 2019 American equivalent of historical criticism

books in Barth's Germany—pornography for pastors that makes you feel titillated and sophisticated while you're reading it, but doesn't help you develop a relationship with God or guide others to a relationship with God through Jesus Christ. I've been feeding my soul with [them] and wondering why my prayers have felt empty and why church work was starting to feel unfulfilling. I am so thankful that God led me to this book.

Barth was a constant companion throughout my renewal leave. I could only read ten pages or so at a time before my brain would get dizzy and my head felt like it was going to explode. I'd put the book down, read something lighter for a while, and then I'd pick Barth back up and read some more. It is not an exaggeration to say that more than any other book I read while on renewal leave, Karl Barth's *The Epistle to the Romans* changed the way that I do ministry.

When I came back from renewal leave, I immediately began planning a sermon series on Romans based on Barth's commentary. You can't preach on Romans using Barth as a guide and be subtle, gentle, or circumspect, so those sermons were particularly pointed and passionate. The change extended beyond that sermon series. Several members of my congregation commented, in the months after my return, that some of the best sermons they'd heard me preach had been ones I'd preached since returning from renewal leave. They said there was a change in my preaching. The most perceptive of them observed that there was a change in *me* as well. The Holy Spirit had filled me with conviction and made me a preacher again, not just a deliverer of sermons.

Who is that author for you? Who is the author who has fascinated you, challenged you, or inspired you? Whose work have you always wanted to read more of? I'm not talking about an author you've used for Bible studies or read with your congregation. You'll have opportunities to do that once your renewal leave is over. I'm talking about someone who will stretch you and take more of your spiritual and mental energy than you can give when you're trying to complete the daily and weekly tasks of ministry. Find a book by that author and make it one of the centerpieces of your renewal leave, along with your Bible. Take it with you wherever you go. Read a little bit at a time and see how the Holy Spirit uses that book and that author to fill your heart.

Don't let this book be the only one you take with you, though. Invest in books—lots of them. If you're on a tight budget, consider buying used books or even borrowing books from the library. On my renewal leave, I sat with Steinbeck under a redwood tree, camped out with Eugene Peterson in a leaky old tent, kept myself up late at night biting my fingernails with Agatha Christie, and rode a train from New Orleans to Memphis with Martin Luther King, Jr. Each of these literary companions fed my soul or opened my mind in some way, making my renewal leave richer and more rewarding.

7) Sit in a pew for a change.

It may be tempting to stay home on Sunday morning during your renewal leave, and I can't blame you if you decide to do that for a while. If your renewal leave is more than a few weeks long, though, chances are good that at some point you're going to miss church. You should absolutely not spend your renewal leave sitting in the pews of the church where you are serving (even though it would be convenient—especially if you live in a parsonage next to the church).

Let me say that again, because it's important to hear: do not spend your renewal leave sitting in the pews of the church you are serving. You need to fully disconnect from your pastoral role for the renewal leave to accomplish what it is intended to accomplish, and your church needs to have the opportunity to fully experience this time without you. If that's uncomfortable to hear, go back and re-read chapter 3 ("I Can't Do This").

At the same time, you will want to attend church somewhere on at least some of the Sundays during your renewal leave. Why not take this opportunity to hear some of your friends preach or listen to some of the well-known preachers that you've always wanted to hear in person? Later in this book, you'll read about a few of my adventures—and misadventures—trying to pack in as many sermons from my friends as possible.

Here's one thing I learned from my experience: you'll make best use of this time if you have at least a rough plan of where you're going to spend your Sunday mornings rather than trying to figure it out each Saturday night. Get out a piece of paper now and write down all the pastors you would like to hear preach during your renewal leave. These could be famous preachers or preachers who are friends of yours, or just people you know about that you've always been curious to hear.

If you're like me, that list will be longer than the number of Sundays during your renewal leave. You can always try a "Sermon-Feast," like I did, but I can tell you from firsthand experience that sometimes being a little bit less ambitious is a good thing. Keep this list and use it as a starting point for planning the Sundays of your next renewal leave.

I packed in a lot during the three months of my renewal leave and learned many lessons along the way. I'm excited to be able to share some of these experiences and discoveries in the pages that follow, and I hope they'll spark some ideas and inspiration for you. Even though the places you go and the experiences you have on your renewal leave will be different than mine, the basic advice mentioned in this chapter should prepare you to have a prosperous, restorative renewal leave that will leave you ready to come back to your church with passion and excitement.

CHAPTER SIX

Building a Budget (and Figuring Out How to Pay for It)

Y ou've decided you're ready to take renewal leave. Your church is in a solid position for their pastor to be away for a while. Your church leadership, your family, and your denominational leadership are all on board. The next big question you're probably asking yourself is, "How am I going to pay for this?"

That question felt daunting as I planned my renewal leave. I had *three whole months* to plan for with no church responsibilities to speak of. The possibilities seemed endless! Our family's savings, however, were not, and I didn't want to use every penny we had stashed away on my renewal leave. A budget was clearly going to be required, and the first step was going to be figuring out how much money I had available to spend.

As I mentioned earlier, there are grants available for pastors who are taking renewal leave. If you get one of these grants that fully funds your renewal leave, you'll probably be asking a different set of questions than I was at this point. Your question might be something

like, "How am I going to spend all this money?!" If that's the question
you're asking yourself, good for you! Answering it will be the fun part
of building a renewal leave budget.

Show Me the Money

If, however, you're cobbling together funding from a variety of sources,
like I was, building the "available resources" side of the budget takes a
little more planning. Again, your context will be different than mine,
so your potential sources of funding will also be different. Here are
some general questions you might want to ask yourself as you're putting together the sources of funds for your upcoming renewal leave.

1) "Could my congregation help fund my renewal leave?"

If you've been working hard and things are going well at your church,
it's not unreasonable to think that your church might fund part of
your renewal leave. Renewal leave is a paid leave in my denomination, so my church contributed to my renewal leave by continuing
to pay my salary and provide benefits while I was away. Even if your
congregation is not able to do this much, you may find them more
willing to help financially than you might initially suppose. After
all, your salary is a matter of public record. Your congregation will
know if you don't make enough money to fully fund a renewal leave
on your own. If they've already agreed that you need this, they will
likely be able to find some way to help you accomplish it.

2) "Are there any resources available from my denomination or association?"

If your church is part of a larger body like a denomination or church association, you may be eligible for grants from that body that are designated for pastors taking renewal leave. Even if there isn't grant money specifically designated for this purpose, you may be able to find grants that could be applied to some specific part of your time away. For example, my denomination doesn't have any grants specifically designated for renewal leave, but they do have grants of up to five hundred dollars available to support pastors' spiritual development. Rather than writing an application focused on my renewal leave as a whole, which would not have qualified for one of these grants, I specifically tailored my application to the portion of my time that would be spent at a monastery, which did qualify. The grant I received did not fully fund my renewal leave, but it got me five hundred dollars closer!

3) "Do I have any other sources of funds that I could apply to my renewal leave?"

This is the part where you'll want to get creative and think about areas where you may have smaller amounts of money coming in that could help fund your renewal leave. If you've been dropping your pocket change into a big bowl for the past five years, now's the time to cash those coins in. Do you typically spend your tax return on a nice meal out as soon as you get it? Not this year! Put it in the bank and use it to help fund your renewal leave. Honoraria from weddings, Christmas gifts from the church, pastor appreciation gifts—none of these individually are all that much, but if you start putting them in a renewal leave savings fund, you'll be surprised how quickly they add up.

As I was looking for ways to save up for my renewal leave, I stumbled onto a way of making money and getting healthy at the same time. Our health insurance provides me with us a pedometer that measures my steps. The more I walk, the more money I get. During the months leading up to my renewal leave, I walked a lot! When my renewal leave began, I cashed in all the rewards I'd earned. I'm not sure which surprised me more—how much healthier I felt, or how much money I'd saved for my renewal leave.

4) "How much money am I able and willing to invest from my own personal resources?"

The sources I've listed above will get you at least part of the way to funding your renewal leave. At some point, though, you're probably going to have to ask yourself how many temporary changes in your own financial plans you're willing to make to fund this. I want to be clear that I do not advocate defaulting on bills or taking loans to fund a renewal leave.

Hopefully, though, you're a smart and savvy pastor who is putting away savings for future expenses like retirement, your next car, next year's vacation, and so forth. Ask yourself whether any of these funds could be temporarily diverted to help with your renewal leave. If you are married and your spouse works, is your spouse able to contribute any of his or her income to your renewal leave budget? Investing for the future is important, but getting yourself back in good health for another decade (or two or three) of ministry is an important investment as well!

5) "Have I prayed about this?"

I don't believe that God responds to our frivolous requests for more money and more belongings. I do, however, believe that God provides what we need. If you've gotten this far, you have already discerned that a renewal leave is necessary for your continued well-being and effectiveness as a pastor. God has ordained your ministry, so if money is the thing that is keeping you from doing this thing that will help your ministry, you have an obligation to go to God with that information and trust God to decide what to do about it.

Toward the end of my renewal leave, I had to sheepishly confess to Julie that I had calculated incorrectly, and that I didn't have enough money to fully cover the final trip of my renewal leave to New Orleans and Memphis. I had not shared this information with anyone else, and I don't believe Julie did, either. Nevertheless, shortly after that conversation, some unexpected money came in from a family member that was more than enough to cover the deficit. Both Julie and I saw God's hand in this seeming coincidence of timing. As Matthew 7:7 says, "Ask, and it will be given you; search, and you will find; knock, and the door will be opened for you."

By now, you've probably realized that funding your renewal leave is a process that isn't going to happen overnight. Searching for funding sources, applying for grants, and saving up honoraria will take some time. Even if you're in a hurry like I was, and you don't want to wait the time it will take to apply for one of the big renewal leave grants, you should still give yourself several months to gather the financial resources you'll need.

It's also a good idea for the resources side of your budget to be a little larger than your anticipated expenses. I've heard it said that when you're starting a building project at a church, you should always plan on it costing 20 percent more than you think. A cushion of 20 percent might be more than you need for your renewal leave budget, but having some extra money to work with will accommodate any unexpected expenses that you didn't think about when you were planning your budget. Hopefully, it will keep you from running out of money before your renewal leave is over, like I almost did!

A cushion will also give you flexibility to be spontaneous or generous when opportunities arise. Driving back to Santa Fe, New Mexico, after my stay at The Monastery of Christ in the Desert, I stopped at a weaver's studio in a small town. I started talking to one of the owners of the studio, who gave me a demonstration on her loom while we discussed the similarities between weaving a tapestry and crafting a sermon (there are more than you might think!). As the shuttle flew from side to side, the weaver told me about one of the young women who showed her work at the studio—a promising artist who had just been getting started in her craft when she was in a serious car accident. This weaver was slowly returning to her art but was struggling to find the confidence she had before her accident. I certainly didn't have a line in my budget for purchasing works of art, but as I thought about the many people who had supported me when I was getting started at my craft of preaching, I knew I wanted to support the young artist by buying one of her weavings. Having a little bit more money available than you plan to spend will allow you to respond when the Holy Spirit weaves opportunities like this into the tapestry of your renewal leave.

Line by Line

The exact details of your budget will depend on how you choose to spend your renewal leave. However, there are some broad categories you'll want to include, as well as some specific questions you'll want to ask as you're putting together your plans. This is by no means an exhaustive list, but it does reflect some of the lessons I learned from putting together my budget that I wanted to share with you.

1) Books

This one is so important to me that I wrote extensively about it in chapter 5! There is enormous value in heavily investing in books for your renewal leave.

2) Food

How important is it to you to eat three full meals a day? When I was traveling, I generally tried to eat at least one proper meal each day, whether at a restaurant or one I prepared myself. I also kept my costs down by eating a granola bar or peanut butter crackers and some dried fruit for one meal most days. This made for a cheap, healthy meal and came with the added advantage of leaving me more time and money for other things that were more important to me on my renewal leave. Bonus tip: If you're booking a hotel, try to choose one that includes breakfast in the cost of the room.

3) Lodging

If you're going to travel much during your renewal leave, it is probably a good idea to stay with friends or family for at least some of the time to keep expenses down. You'll also want to spend some time on your own, so at some point you'll need to budget for lodging. As you do, consider how much luxury you really require. That four-star hotel might look great, but can you stay in something a little more modest and use the savings to fund another part of your renewal leave? Airbnb or a similar rental service can be a convenient and reasonably priced option if you're only staying somewhere for a night or two. If you're going to be staying for a week or longer, consider a cabin or a weekly rental as another way of minimizing costs. If you're the outdoorsy type, consider camping in a tent. State parks are often a good bet for high-quality, low-cost campsites. If you can schedule a camping trip while schools are in session, you may be able to find a campground where the only occupants are you and the local wildlife!

4) Music

Music has the power to evoke memories of an event long after the event is over. You might purchase an album or a few songs that relate to each part of your renewal leave, or create a renewal leave-themed playlist on a music streaming service. I made playlists for most of my trips, selecting music that related to what I'd be doing and the people who would be with me. Even now, long after my renewal leave is over, when I listen to one of those playlists it reminds me of all the fun adventures I had. If you're a musician, consider taking your instrument with you. I play the piano, which isn't very portable, but more than once I found myself sitting beside a campfire wishing I knew how to play the harmonica!

5) Stipend for a pulpit-supply preacher

This is something you'll need to work out with your congregation. If you serve a church with multiple clergy on staff, it may not even be an issue. If you are your church's only pastor, though, you'll need to have a plan for covering preaching and other pastoral duties. Will congregation members fill these roles or will you bring in someone from outside? If you bring someone in, will you give them a stipend for their services? (The answer to that question should be yes, by the way.) If you give them a stipend, how much of that will you pay, and how much will the church pay? Together, you and your church leadership should agree on the answers to these questions well in advance of your renewal leave.

6) Thank you gifts

This is an essential line item in your budget. After we arrived home from Michigan with a borrowed GPS that belonged to a generous five-and-dime owner (don't worry, that story is coming), I sent the GPS back north in a box along with a sweatshirt from our town's own historic five-and-dime. After staying with two pastors who'd been long-time mentors, I sent some dried cherries from an orchard in Julie's hometown to each of them. While none of the thank-you gifts I sent cost much individually, together they added up. Even so, they were a small price to pay to express my gratitude for all the generosity I received during my renewal leave!

7) Transportation

This is where you can really get creative to keep costs down—or where you can burn a lot of your budget if you're not careful. Air travel is convenient and quick, but it's expensive. You're on renewal leave! Do you need to get everywhere as quickly as possible? Greyhound and other bus services offer low-cost transportation to almost anywhere in the country. Amtrak offers a few more amenities, and a train ride can make any trip feel like an adventure. If you're really on a tight budget, you might be able to find family members or clergy colleagues who would be willing to give you a ride. Finally, a reliable car can get you just about anywhere you want to go. Just don't forget to budget for gas!

8) Travel Insurance

To buy, or not to buy? That is the question. I bought travel insurance for my trip to New Mexico because it involved two plane trips, a rental car, and some nonrefundable money paid in advance for lodging. With other trips, I took my chances. You'll have to decide for yourself how much risk you're willing to live with. If you've kept your expenses down, you shouldn't lose too much money even if you can't avoid canceling a trip.

9) Miscellaneous

Undoubtedly, you'll have more categories depending on your interests, your needs, and the unique way you're planning to spend your renewal leave. Make sure you budget for some of the things that bring you joy! I love taking pictures with my old 35mm film camera, so I budgeted for film and developing. Don't forget to put something in your budget for souvenirs, parking, and admission fees.

Also, don't budget every penny available for your renewal leave. Unexpected expenses will come up! For example, I ended up needing to rent a car after one of our cars unexpectedly stopped working. That was *definitely* not in my budget. It's good to have some wiggle room for moments like that, so a crisis doesn't become a financial catastrophe that prevents you from continuing your renewal leave.

You can't possibly plan or budget for everything that will happen on your renewal leave—and you wouldn't want to if you could. Part of the excitement of renewal leave is giving yourself over to God's leading by removing the carefully scheduled obligations from your life, then seeing where the Holy Spirit takes you. Having a basic budget in place, though, will reduce your stress and give you permission to spend money on the things you've budgeted for. It will also give you a framework for discerning whether the opportunities that present themselves are an expensive distraction you should avoid, or whether it just might be the Holy Spirit leading you on an exciting and unexpected renewal leave adventure you'll never forget!

CHAPTER SEVEN

Before You Leave, Plan Your Return

I get it, I really do. You've got an impossibly long list of things you need to accomplish before you can start your renewal leave—not to mention all your regular responsibilities—and I have the audacity to suggest that you should plan for your return *before* you even leave! You may be asking yourself if I even realize what it's like to plan a renewal leave in the middle of an exhausting church schedule.

Yes, I do. I also know what it's like to come back from renewal leave and hit the ground running. While you're away on renewal leave, your church will be eagerly awaiting your return. The more you can do ahead of time to plan your first Sunday back, the richer the experience will be for your congregation, and the more stress-free it will be for you.

The first and most important thing to remember is that while you're spending several months away on renewal leave having life-changing and call-restoring experiences, your church will be having their own equally important experiences. If the same preacher has filled the pulpit throughout your renewal leave, your congregation will have developed an important relationship with that person. Your first Sunday back is an opportunity for your church to celebrate and acknowledge their experiences during the time you were away, and for you to acknowledge the importance of those experiences.

The second thing to remember is that, while your congregation will want to hear about your time away, they don't need to hear everything on the first Sunday you're back. You will want to share all the things you've learned and all the ways you've grown, and you'll have plenty of time to do that in the weeks and months to come. Spread out those insights and the things you've learned. Sprinkle them into sermons, Bible studies, and pastoral conversations over time. You may find that your own understanding of what you have learned and experienced will deepen over the weeks and months following your renewal leave, and you'll have even more enriching things to offer your congregation after a period of reflection.

The final important point to remember is that your first Sunday back should be a day of celebration! Before you leave, work with your Renewal Leave Team to plan something fun and out of the ordinary. My church organized a pitch-in dinner and talent show, which was just right for us. You might choose a more formal time to share about your experiences on renewal leave, either on one of your first Sundays back or in the weeks that follow it. However, try not to schedule too much for that first Sunday afternoon . . . other than maybe a nap!

In the appendix at the back of this book, you'll find a liturgy in four parts: 1) for sending a pastor into renewal leave; 2) for receiving a pastor as pulpit supply; 3) for sending a pastor for pulpit supply at the end of a renewal leave; and 4) for receiving a pastor back from renewal leave. My church used this liturgy in the worship services at either end of my renewal leave and found it to be helpful. I hope that yours will as well.

†††
PART THREE

The Pastor Takes a Leave

CHAPTER EIGHT

Reading *East of Eden* West of the Rockies

S alinas, California, in June is a study in contrasts. If you look in one direction, you'll see giant boulders jutting out of the hills amidst a sea of dormant brown grass. If you look in the other, you'll see lush, irrigated fields filled with row after row of fresh vegetables. If you listen carefully, you'll imagine you can hear the sound of the ocean a few miles to the west. We had stopped on the outskirts of Salinas because I'd convinced Julie to take a several-miles-long detour as we drove from Los Angeles to Monterey. I was reading *East of Eden*, which Steinbeck set in his hometown of Salinas, and I wanted to see the place for myself.

Every summer, Julie, the boys, and I take a two-week trip to get away from the pressures of church, school, and everyday life. The trip always involves relaxation, adventure, and new experiences. Most years, it involves a tent in the middle of a forest, but if we have family or friends who live in the direction we're planning to go, we'll sometimes stop by for a visit. This year, we decided we would begin our vacation at the annual gathering of my mom's family in Las Vegas, Nevada.

As a pastor, telling your congregation that you're taking your family (including your relatively young children) to Las Vegas on vacation is an interesting experience. Eyebrows raise and questioning glances are exchanged. You can almost hear the thoughts rattling around in the parishioners' minds: "Sin City? What happens in Vegas, stays in Vegas, doesn't it? What do we not know about our pastor?"

I've now had this experience in multiple churches, and I can safely tell you that eyebrows quickly settle back to their regular location once I explain *why* we're going to Las Vegas. Several members of my mom's family live on the West Coast. Others live in the Desert Southwest. The rest of us live in the Midwest. Las Vegas happens to be a convenient middle ground for our family, and there are always cheap, easy flights from everywhere that the family lives. It helps that the city has relatively inexpensive lodging, and, while Julie and I don't gamble, my grandmother used to enjoy playing the dollar slots. Having the reunion in Las Vegas was the best way we could ensure that Grandma would make an appearance every year! After her death, our family decided to continue the tradition.

As we were deciding where to take our family vacation—a trip that would double as the first trip of my renewal leave—it made sense to start in Las Vegas. Spending time with family is important to us, and since it had been several years since we'd been to the reunion, there were family members we hadn't seen for quite a while. We ultimately decided to fly our camping gear out with us, spend a few days in Las Vegas catching up with relatives, and then head out in a rental car to a campground somewhere along the coast for the rest of our vacation.

A family reunion turned out to be a perfect way to start the traveling part of my renewal leave. We spent several glorious days by the hotel pool, basking in the desert sun while we caught up with relatives. Everybody brings their favorite snack when they come to the reunion, and since it just wouldn't be polite to refuse someone when they invite you to share their favorite snack with you, we filled our bellies with treats. My mom's side of the family has deep Irish roots and the storytelling tradition that comes along with those roots, so we laughed until we couldn't laugh anymore at all the stories we never get tired of telling or hearing—many of which involve family members who are no longer with us. We shed some tears along with the laughter as we remembered loved ones who used to come to the reunion but are gone now.

A friend of mine once described the particular phase of life she was in as the "sweet spot." Her children were old enough that they didn't require constant care, yet young enough to enjoy being with their parents and each other. Her parents and others of their generation were still alive and healthy. As I lounged around the pool, gobbling down chips and cookies with my family while aunts and uncles told their favorite stories from times gone by, I realized that I was living in the sweet spot my friend had described, and it made me deeply grateful.

In *East of Eden,* Steinbeck describes the cycles of rain and drought, of plenty and hunger, that shaped life in the part of California where he grew up. He writes that "during the dry years people forgot about the rich years, and during the wet years they lost all memory of the dry years. It was always that way."[1] As I read those words while sitting among people I loved, they resonated with me. There have been years that weren't as sweet as this one. There were years when we flew out west for a funeral instead of the family reunion. I know there will

---

1. John Steinbeck, *East of Eden* (New York: The Viking Press, 2003), p. 6.

be more years like that—dry years when our family gatherings produce more tears than laughter. This wasn't one of those years, though, and I was grateful for the days spent with family during one of the "sweet spots" of life.

After a few days in Vegas, we packed our camping gear in our rental car and headed north toward Monterey and Santa Cruz for the remainder of our vacation. Having visited Monterey as a child, I remembered the Monterey Bay Aquarium as a magical place full of awe and wonder, and I wanted my kids to see it for themselves. I hoped it was actually as good as it was in my memories and in the stories I'd told my kids. Otherwise, we were all going to be disappointed.

You know how a lot of treasured places from your childhood seem a little less grand and less impressive when you revisit them as an adult? That was not the case for the Monterey Bay Aquarium! It was every bit as good as I remembered it. Huge schools of shimmering silver fish darted through kelp forests in massive saltwater aquariums. We watched as bottom-dwelling fish buried themselves in sand waiting for an unwitting shrimp to wander by and become dinner. The abundance of sea life in the building amazed us, yet we knew it was only a small sampling of the diversity that could be found in the water just beyond the seashore. Aside from one *minor* disappointment—the ethereal voice of Sigourney Weaver only welcomes visitors to the Aquarium in the movie *Finding Dory* and not in real life—we all ranked the aquarium as even better than expected.

After a delicious fish dinner on the docks of Monterey, during which we tried not to think too hard about the irony of what we were eating, we made our way to Santa Cruz for the remainder of our family vacation. If you happen to be looking for a place to really kick off your renewal leave, you could hardly pick a better spot than

Santa Cruz. Our campsite was at the edge of a forest populated by giant redwoods—the tallest trees in the world and a genuine wonder to behold. We pitched our tent under a tree so tall we had to tip our necks all the way back, bend our backs, and strain our eyes to see the top of it. Our youngest son discovered a hollowed-out redwood stump, which became a makeshift fort for the four of us to play in and hold family meetings where we talked about vitally important, vacation-y topics. We spent the first day or so hiking among the redwoods, enjoying the forest, and looking for banana slugs—giant, fluorescent-yellow critters that dwell in the redwoods and were a source of fascination to three of us while completely grossing out the fourth (though I'll never tell who was who!)

We could easily have spent our entire time in California roaming around the forest searching for massive mollusks crawling on gargantuan trees, but the redwood forests aren't all that Santa Cruz has to offer. After spending a few days among the trees, we headed to the beach to take in the sun and the surf. We dug our toes into the sand, listened to the cries of the seagulls, and went deep sea fishing where we caught so many fish we had to give some away. It turns out that there's nothing that soothes my soul quite like returning from a day on the water with the people I love to a redwood-shaded campsite, eating fish we caught together and cooked over a campfire we built.

While I played hard during my time in Santa Cruz, I never forgot my other purpose for being there. This was vacation, but it was also renewal leave. While I was relaxing, I also had some deep spiritual work to do, and *East of Eden* continued to be a source of insight for me. Steinbeck's semi-autographical novel is also a dramatic retelling of the story of Cain and Abel set in the place the author knew best. The characters in the book wrestle with the reality of sin and the human tug-of-war between doing the right thing and doing the wrong one, between taking the easy choice that leads to bad results or the hard choice that leads to something better. Through countless choices the characters make, both good and bad, Steinbeck makes it clear that the most important thing is that we always have a choice.

I didn't miss the connection to my own situation. I had the choice to continue giving insufficient attention to prayer, family, and rest until I either limped my way to retirement or crashed and burned. I could do that; I'd seen other pastors do it before. Or, I could choose a different, healthier, holier, and more balanced approach—a way that would begin among the redwoods and sandy beaches of Santa Cruz and develop over the next three months of renewal leave.

Whatever choice I made would not just affect me and my family; it would affect my congregation as well. It is not a blessing for a congregation to have a pastor whose wheels are constantly spinning and whose spiritual tank is always running on empty. It is not a blessing for a pastor to work hard at the tasks of ministry but neglect the deeper spiritual practices that inform those tasks and make them life-giving for pastor and congregation alike. It's not a recipe for good sermons, for attentive and capable pastoral care, or for a pastor who can serve as a good example in living a healthy spiritual life.

Thankfully, this dire outcome is not an inevitable evolution of the call to ministry. I came to an important realization under the redwoods that the bright flame that had beckoned me into ministry didn't have to slowly dwindle into nothingness until it eventually burned out. There was another way—a way I had once known but slowly lost sight of—a way that involved making good decisions and taking time away from the hectic nature of church ministry to focus on God and family.

While there were many ways I could have started my three months away from church ministry, choosing to spend those early days basking in the love of family as I reclaimed a sense of holy rest set the tone for everything else that would come. The bright neon lights of Las Vegas and the warm glow of the campfire had begun to illuminate a path I had nearly left behind as the tasks of ministry distracted me from the deeper spiritual responsibilities of prayer and rest.

Now I had three months to find my way back to that path.

CHAPTER NINE

If We Don't Have It, You Don't Need It

I've never understood why people make mother-in-law jokes. I guess it works for some people, but I've had a very different experience with my in-laws. Both Julie and I were blessed to marry into families that we like and who like each other. Julie sometimes goes shopping with my mom just for fun. When Julie's parents are coming for a visit, I look forward to it for weeks. In fact, our parents sometimes plan their vacations so they can hang out with each other even when we're not going to be around! That's why, when Julie's mom and dad asked me if I'd be visiting them as part of my renewal leave, I immediately said, "You bet."

Early in my planning, I decided that a week-long, one-on-one trip with each of our boys was a top priority for my renewal leave travels. There are many advantages to life as a pastor's kid (leftover chicken from church meals being at the top of both our boys' lists), but there are also some big downsides. The inability to ever take weekend trips as a family is definitely one of them.

Unlike a lot of families who have their weekends off, we just don't get to take short trips together. A pastor's family can't decide on the spur of the moment to leave home on a Friday evening and come back Sunday night. When other families are packing their bags to take advantage of an extended holiday weekend, I'm still revising my sermon for Sunday morning. As a result, whenever I have a week off, all four of us take a trip as a family—the time is simply too precious to consider spending any other way. Julie's work schedule allows her to occasionally take one or the other of our boys to her parents' house for the weekend, but I couldn't remember ever taking a trip by myself with just one of our children. That's why, when I knew I would have three months without Sunday morning obligations, the thing I most wanted was a whole week traveling with just our thirteen-year-old and a whole week traveling with just our seven-year-old. A one-on-one road trip with each kid sounded great.

Fishing and Picking Cherries in Northern Michigan

The length of the trip was a particular challenge when planning an excursion with my younger son. A week would be a long time for him to be away from home and the rest of the family, especially his mom. A shorter trip might have been a better idea, but our sons are competitive, and I knew there would be grumbling if the thirteen-year-old got a longer trip than his little brother. Instead, what our seven-year-old really needed was a place that felt almost as comfortable as his own home where he would be surrounded by people he loved as much as his parents. A visit to northern Michigan and a week of outdoor fun with Grandma and Grandpa was the perfect solution.

I would never recommend picking your spouse based on where their parents live. But, *if* you were determined to marry someone based on where you'd be spending the holidays, I'd recommend looking for someone from northern Michigan. Julie's parents live in a postcard-perfect village surrounded by pine forests and cherry orchards. Their house is just a few minutes down the road from a crystal-clear lake with a great beach. It's an easy drive from Lake Michigan. There's no movie theater, no Wal-Mart, no bowling alley, and no shopping mall anywhere near their house. Instead, there are trees, hills, lakes, deer, fish, and a whole lot of snow in the winter.

When the snow covers the ground, people ski and ice fish and ride snowmobiles. During the summer months, they hike, fish, go boating, and pick cherries. When you come visit with their grand-child for a week, they pack in as many of these wonderful northern Michigan activities into your time with them as they possibly can.

The week was nonstop fun, with every day bringing new adven-tures. Two moments, though, will remain with me for a long time. The first took place on a bridge over a creek just outside the village where Julie's parents live. The weather was perfect for fishing and a warm summer breeze made ripples on the sun-dappled water. My son and his young cousins cast line after line into the stream, trying to catch the "big grandpappy fish" rumored to live in the deep waters beneath the bridge. Try as we might, nobody caught it that day. We did, however, lose a lot of bobbers in the weeds that grow in the shal-low water.

As were fishing, I happened to look over at my father-in-law when another bright yellow bobber went floating down the creek. He was tying a bobber to a fishing line for what must have been the twentieth time that day, and I saw him glance in the water as the twenty-first slowly drifted out of view. Was he frustrated, though? Far from it. He looked like a guy who couldn't imagine anything he'd rather be doing than tying bobbers on his grandchildren's fishing lines all day long. Maybe he couldn't.

The second moment I'll long remember took place in a cherry orchard not far from the house where Julie grew up. Unlike some fruits, non-organic cherries only require a small amount of pesticide, which is applied at the beginning of the season. By the time they're ready to pick, the pesticide has completely washed off in the rain. As a non-Michigander, I was astonished to learn that the only spray lingering on sweet cherries at picking time is . . . sugar! Yep, the only residue left on sweet cherries when you pick them is not only non-toxic, but also makes them even more delicious. Unsurprisingly, people tend to pop a few cherries in their mouth as they're picking—which the orchard owners don't seem to mind too much.

One day during our visit, Julie's mom took us cherry picking at an orchard her family used to own. Heavy clusters of deep red cherries dangled from the orderly rows of trees lining the orchard. While we picked cherries, my mother-in-law told us how Julie's great-grandmother had been picking cherries in that very orchard on the day she went into labor with Julie's grandmother. The sense of family history and the ties to the land could not have been more profound.

My wife loves Michigan cherries more than just about any other food, so I was on a mission to pick lots of cherries to bring back home to her. My mother-in-law was, too. Her grandson, however, had a different agenda. His goal was to stuff as many cherries into his face as he possibly could! I will long remember the sight of my mother-in-law picking cherries like a pro and dropping into her bucket by the handful, while my son had maybe seven cherries at the bottom of his bucket and cherry juice streaming down his chin. I don't know whose grin was bigger.

The week we spent with Julie's parents was a treat for our youngest son, who usually has to "share" his grandma and grandpa with his brother. He basked in their undivided attention all week long. Seeing the look on his face when he pulled a fish out of the water, and, later, when he proudly presented his mom with all cherries he'd picked himself (sort of), I knew I'd made the right decision about where to take him on our trip. He will always remember the week he spent in northern Michigan with his grandma and grandpa—and he's not the only one. Spending that week with them was a treat for me, too.

When my in-laws come to visit, they usually stay for a few days at a time, often coming in on a Friday evening and leaving on Monday morning. As a pastor, those are the days I have the least flexibility in my schedule. There are few things I enjoy more than having either my parents or Julie's parents at church with us on Sunday, but I'm often so busy practicing my sermon, communicating with the tech team, and getting updates on the status of parishioners' relatives that I only connect with them in passing at the church. If there's a wedding or a funeral scheduled on Saturday, I can't postpone those events because my in-laws are in town. As they get in the car to drive home, I often find myself feeling unsatisfied with the amount of time I've been able to spend with them.

Being on renewal leave meant that I was able to be fully present with Julie's parents for the whole time I was with them. During that week in northern Michigan, I was able to reclaim some relationship-building time that pastoral commitments and bad timing had taken away over the years. I planned a week with my in-laws to accommodate a seven-year-old's need for familiarity away from home, but it turned out to be just as much a blessing to me as it was to him.

We Needed It, They Had It

Our week in northern Michigan went off without a hitch. The drive back? Not so much. In fact, were it not for the generosity of strangers, we might have been at my in-laws' house far longer than originally anticipated.

Julie and I tend to drive cars until they won't run anymore. That's partly a financial decision, but it also fits with our general life philosophy of using stuff to the very end rather than replacing something that still works. In practical terms, it meant that both our cars were well broken in at the time of my renewal leave. This meant that one way or another, I was going to drive up to Michigan in an old car. Julie's car had about 200,000 miles on it, but it got better gas mileage than mine did, so that's the one I chose for our trip. The car did just fine on the drive to Julie's parents' house. It was the drive home at the end of the trip that was a problem.

I had just pulled out of the driveway at Julie's parents' house to start a full day of driving when the speedometer on the dashboard display disappeared. A minute later, the fuel gauge readout vanished as well. When I tried to back up, the backup camera didn't come on either. I was beginning to get the sense that I was in big trouble.

I took the car to a nearby repair shop. The owner took a quick look at the car and spent a few minutes clicking around on his computer. When he looked up, the pitying look on his face told me the news was not going to be good.

"Is it really bad?" I asked.

He nodded. "I can't help you," he said.

"I have to get home," I responded plaintively.

"Where's home?"

"Southern Indiana."

"That's a long way," he said offering me another pitying look.

"Here's what you can do," he finally told me. "You should be able to make it home before the car completely shuts down. The speedometer's shot, so you'll need to find some way to tell how fast you're going. You'll need to stop for gas before you think you need to since you don't have a gas gauge. Don't turn the car on and off any more than you absolutely need to. As soon as you get home, drive the car to a dealership and see how much you can get for it as a trade-in. Whatever they offer, take it."

This was better news than it could have been. In theory it meant we'd still be able to get home. The speedometer was an issue, though. At the time, I didn't carry a smart phone with me,[1] which would have had a speedometer app on it. There was a GPS built into the car, but it was a casualty of the electrical system shutting down. We didn't have a portable GPS device because with the car's built-in GPS, we didn't need one. I asked the guy at the auto repair shop if he sold a portable speedometer. No luck, and, as he pointed out, there wasn't a Wal-Mart for about twenty-five miles.

I was stumped. It looked like we might well be stuck in town for a while, and we really needed to get home. I had one last idea, though, and while it was a long shot, I thought it just might work. There's an old five-and-dime store in the village that's been open for years and has a reputation for carrying things that you can't get anywhere else. I knew that if anybody in town had a portable speedometer or something like it, they would. So, I decided to find out.

I walked through the door and announced, "I hear your motto is 'If we don't have it, you don't need it.'"

---

1. I know, I know!

The folks behind the counter chuckled knowingly. Apparently, I wasn't the first person to use that line. One of them said, "I get the feeling you're about to put that to the test."

I said, "I need a portable speedometer." I explained the whole situation and while they sympathized with my predicament, they didn't have one.

This is where things got really cool. The people working at the five-and-dime store called around to auto parts stores in all the towns that I might have been able to reach without getting pulled over for accidentally breaking the speed limit. Nobody carried a portable speedometer. I was out of luck once again. I knew the five-and-dime had been a long shot, but it was worth a try. I thanked the clerks behind the counter and was moving toward the door when the owner said, "Keep the gentleman here for a minute," and walked purpose-fully out the shop's back door.

A few minutes later, she came in holding a portable GPS that looked like it had just come from someone's dashboard. As it turned out, it had come off of hers. "I don't really go anywhere," she said. "If you promise to send it back, you can use my GPS."

I was blown away. This was a total stranger who didn't know any-thing about me, and here she was giving me her portable GPS to take to another state, trusting that I would eventually send it back.

As a pastor, I'm accustomed to being on the giving side of situa-tions of need. I do a lot of problem solving in my ministry. I support others a lot. When I read Jesus' parable about the Good Samaritan, I typically read it as a reminder to be like the Samaritan, who stops and offers help, rather than the priest and the Levite, who cross to the other side of the road and hurry on their way. I rarely picture myself in the role of the man on the side of the road who needs help.

This changed during the three months of my renewal leave. I found myself dependent on the generosity of others time and again. I stayed in other people's homes. I ate other people's food. I often relied on strangers for help, directions, and advice. And once, I borrowed a stranger's GPS to get my seven-year-old home to see his mom.

My road to renewal included a rekindled awareness that I'm not in charge of my life nearly as much as I think I am. Far from being the proverbial lone ranger, I exist inside a complex network of generosity, support, and mutuality. I needed a reminder that deepening my relationship with God includes growing my relationships with others, whether these are people I am already close to or former strangers who become friends through moments of generosity and kindness.

I found these reminders everywhere during our week in northern Michigan: on a bridge shadowing the watery lair of an elusive grandpappy fish; in the neat rows of cherry trees ripe for the picking (and eating); and in the unexpected generosity of a five-and-dime store owner who acted as a neighbor to a stranger and his young son, in need and far away from home.

† † †
The Good Samaritan (From a Different Point of View)

Pick up a Bible and turn to Luke 10. Find the parable of the Good Samaritan. Read it through entirely. Now, read it through again. Then, answer these questions:

- Which character(s) do you most identify with?
- How easy, or hard, is it for you to see yourself in the role of the Good Samaritan?
- When you think about taking renewal leave, is it challenging for you to know that you would need to rely on the generosity of others during this time? If so, could this reveal an opportunity for you to grow during your renewal leave as your practice receiving from others with grace and humility?

CHAPTER TEN

Some Things Are More Important (Than Your Budget)

Eventually, we made it back from Michigan safely with help from the borrowed GPS. With only twenty-four hours until my next trip, however, there wasn't time to trade in Julie's car like the repair shop owner had suggested. I also couldn't take my car, which was now our family's only reliably working vehicle, so I got online and found a deal on a rental car. Several loads of laundry later, our thirteen-year-old and I hopped in the rented car and headed south.

A week with my in-laws was the perfect trip for our seven-year-old. He needed a familiar place and familiar faces if he was going to be away from home for that long. With our thirteen-year-old, though, there was no such concern. He was at an age when adventure, new experiences, and nonstop fun were his top priorities. In my mind, this pointed to an obvious destination: Orlando, home of Disney World and Universal Studios!

This would be a once-in-a-lifetime trip. In five years, Julie and I would likely be dropping our firstborn off at college. He and I would probably not have another chance to take a long trip by ourselves before then. Tight budget or not, the circumstances warranted a big, memory-making week. I visited a travel agent several months before my renewal leave began and booked an all-inclusive package with park tickets, lodging, and meals. I'll confess, my eyes went a bit wide when I saw the quote for the trip. I was still trying to figure out exactly how I would pay for all the things I was planning during my three months of leave, even without the trip to Orlando. My eyes got even wider when the travel agent told me the price she'd quoted was just the down payment!

This trip with my son would be the first of several extravagances in my otherwise penny-pinching renewal leave budget. In general, I placed a high value on thriftiness during my renewal leave, trying to save money where I could. There were a few situations, however, when the additional cost justified the expense because it lined up with a value of mine. For instance, on my way back from a monastery in New Mexico, I went significantly over budget to purchase a weaving created by a young artist trying to get back to her craft after a serious car accident shattered her confidence as well as the bones in her leg. Similarly, to celebrate Julie's birthday in the mountains of North Carolina, I paid so much for the only cake I could find in a nearby town that I carried it in a cooler for the rest of the trip and ate a slice every day rather than throw it away and waste a single bite!

Supporting the young weaver became for me a symbolic acknowledgement of the many people who supported me when I was starting out as a young pastor. Julie's birthday cake was a way to show her that my renewal leave didn't eclipse important milestones in her life, like her birthday. As for the trip to Florida, it was an acknowledgement of a fleeting moment in my life as a dad that I needed to capture while I still could.

SOME THINGS ARE MORE IMPORTANT (THAN YOUR BUDGET)   101

Road Trip Songs

I can say without hesitation that the trip was worth every penny. We
had nonstop fun for an entire week. As a teenager, our oldest child
spends a lot of time with his music turned on, earbuds in, and family
tuned out. For this trip, I told him he could bring his music, but he
couldn't use his earbuds in the car. What one of us listened to, both
of us would listen to. While I knew this would cramp my traveling
companion's style a little, it turned out to be an excellent rule for our
trip. Sitting in the car for two days while listening to his favorite
music and podcasts with his dad, our thirteen-year-old was willing
to open up and share some things about his life, his feelings, and his
friends that he'd never told me before. The miles and hours flew by as
we talked to each other, just father and son.

In addition to the music and podcasts, we also had a dedicated
playlist for the trip—the first of several I would make for my various
renewal leave travels, each one themed around the places I was going
and the people I'd be with there. When I asked our seven-year-old
what music he wanted for the drive to Michigan and back, he listed
several albums in their entirety. That was a simple request to fulfill—I
just threw a bunch of CDs in the car and off we went. However, when
I asked our thirteen-year-old what he wanted to listen to, he named
a bunch of unrelated songs that would be impossible to find across
several albums, let alone one or two. Beyond his surprisingly eclectic
taste in music, I was also deeply touched by some of his choices.

Julie started seminary when our oldest son was two years old. She
had heard the call to ministry during my final year of seminary but
she wasn't ready to start back to school right away. After I'd been in
church ministry for a few years, Julie probably would have been ready
to enroll in classes, but then our son was born, and she decided to

wait. By the time he was two, God's tug on Julie's life was so strong that she couldn't ignore it anymore. The seminary that was right for her was several hours from our home, so she would wake up early in the morning, drive to school, and then stay for either one or two nights a week depending on her schedule that semester. When she was done with classes, she would drive back home. It was not the ideal situation, but she persevered and graduated with honors.

In the meantime, I was often home by myself with a young child and a church to care for. Suffice it to say, I have tremendous appreciation and respect for single parents after having just a taste of that life. I know our son got more than his fair share of cranky dad when I picked him up from the babysitter's house after a full day of church work. There were hard moments during those years, for sure, but our son and I were also able to bond in ways that we would not have otherwise.

Some of my favorite memories from those years are the hours we spent rolling back and forth on the parsonage floor, giggling uncontrollably, and bumping into each other while we listened to toddler songs and shouted, "Roll over, roll over!" He came with me on pastoral visits and knew which of the church's homebound members was likely to have candy or a snack cake for him when we arrived. Some of the songs he listed for our trip were ones we'd listened to while we drove to those visits. Others were songs I'd sung to him at night while I rocked him to sleep. I didn't even realize he remembered all the songs he requested for our trip! Just throwing a bunch of CDs in the car clearly would not fully honor this moment.

Instead, I thought about the thirteen years I'd been blessed to be his dad. I thought about the music that made up the soundtrack of our life together to this point. Then, I made a playlist out of the music from our shared experiences. I included a song from his favorite album when he was little, a tune from a Disney movie we'd watched together over and over again, and a Harry Belafonte number I used to sing to him when I was rocking him to sleep. I added a few songs that reflected my observations of his early teenage years, a time of growing independence and questioning of the way his mom and I taught him to do things. I also threw in a couple of sentimental tunes about dads and sons which he probably won't fully appreciate until he's quite a bit older. I'll admit I got a little teary-eyed as I put the playlist together! We started each of our days in the car by listening to that playlist, and we still listen to it from time to time. It brings up a flurry of stories and shared memories from our trip to Florida every time we do.

Finding Magic in Orlando

I booked us at a Disney hotel that was themed around New Orleans' French Quarter and we made it our mission to have fun as soon as we set foot on the property. We splashed and swam in the hotel pool in the shadow of a giant sea monster-shaped slide. We ate Cajun food and Mickey Mouse beignets amid the Mardi Gras décor in the hotel restaurant as jazz music played in the background. In the evenings, I would go for a quick run along the footpaths of the perfectly mani-cured property while my son relaxed in the hotel room with his music and his books. Even if we'd never left the grounds of the hotel, it still would have been a great trip.

Of course, we did leave the hotel. The parks were beckoning and we had come to play. First on our list was the Magic Kingdom, the part of Disney World that probably comes to mind first when you think of Disney parks. We munched on Mickey Mouse-shaped ice cream bars while we waited in line for the Haunted Mansion. We sang along as we rode the Pirates of the Caribbean and It's a Small

World rides (okay, I sang along while my son rolled his eyes). We rode Thunder Mountain, a roller coaster billed as "the wildest ride in the wilderness," holding our hands high over our heads the whole time. We took full advantage of staying at a Disney hotel by heading back during the hottest part of the day and returning to the park after dinner to enjoy more rides well into the night. During one afternoon break, I texted Julie a picture of her not-so-little kid sprawled out on his bed, with his earbuds in and a big grin on his face, resting up before we headed back to the park for more fun.

The next day was dedicated to Epcot, a futuristic (if somewhat dated) look at what progress can do for our lives. My son has always had an interest in science and engineering, so the subject matter of Epcot intrigued him. Since there are more exhibits and fewer rides compared to the Magic Kingdom, the day was a little calmer than the day before. We learned about hydroponic gardening, sampled food from several different countries, soared across desert and mountain landscapes, and came back to the hotel with a build-your-own light-saber. Both the teenager and the middle-aged dad appreciated this relatively "slow day" of education and food with the occasional ride tossed in as well.

The next morning, we checked out of our hotel, waved goodbye to Mickey, and moved down the road to Universal Studios. When my son was younger, we would read Harry Potter books together each year so we decided to spend a whole day on the Harry Potter-themed sections of the park. We'd heard it was almost like spending a day inside a Harry Potter book. Little did we know how true that would be!

At the time, there was a new Potter-related ride that people had been waiting in line for up to eight hours to ride on the busiest days.[1]

---

1. No, that's not a typo, there were eight-hour long lines.

We both agreed we didn't want to wait for eight hours, but we also knew we might not get back to Universal Studios anytime soon and we really wanted to try out this ride. We finally decided on a compromise. We would get in line if the wait was three and a half hours or less. When we arrived at the entrance to the ride, the sign said the wait was three hours, which was within our limit, so we decided to give it a try.

The sky had been pouring rain all morning—I'm talking monsoon-level wet from the time we woke up—and the rain was causing operational issues for the roller coaster. Every so often, we'd hear an announcement that the ride was shutting down temporarily. The coaster cars would be silent for twenty minutes or so and the line wouldn't move. Then, we'd hear the cheers and screams of exhilarated riders for a few minutes while the line crept forward. Before long, though, the familiar announcement would play and the ride was shut down once again.

Another visitor to the park told us that this was a common occurrence, and that the most important thing was to stay in line. If the ride was having too many problems, it would shut down altogether. Everyone who had waited patiently would get a special pass to go to the front of the line when the ride opened again. If you'd given up and gotten out of line, though, you were out of luck.

After two and a half hours of waiting in line without making much forward progress, we were both starting to get hungry. Due to the extremely long wait time, the park had devised a system where you could get out of line for a few minutes to use the bathroom. I got a pass from a line attendant and went to grab some snacks for the two of us.

When I returned five minutes later, snacks in hand, I saw hundreds of people streaming out the exit gate. The ride had shut down completely and there was a man at the exit handing out the special return passes to everyone who waited. My son came up to me carrying one of the special passes and brimming with stories about the elaborate animatronic scenes from the Harry Potter movies inside the building—a classroom, a workshop, and more. Everyone who waited in line had seen it all as they walked toward the exit, except for me.

As I traded in my bathroom pass for one of the special return passes, I explained my situation to the man who was handing out the passes. I knew it was a long shot, but I was hoping my son and I could take a quick walk through the line so I could see the animatronics. We promised to come right back.

The park official started to tell us all the reasons this plan just wouldn't work. It wasn't really his ride. He wasn't even from the same department. Besides, it wasn't safe for us to walk through the ride by ourselves while it was shut down. All the explanations he gave were perfectly reasonable and understandable.

Then, the man stopped abruptly. He looked at the ride operators sitting around without anything to do while the ride was closed, and then turned to us and said, "Well, I mean. . . . I guess we could ask them." He walked up to one of the operators, explained the situation, and asked if any of them had time to walk us through the line. The operator responded, "Why don't you just do it?" and handed him a key, explaining how to use it to turn on all the animatronic scenes. This park employee we'd been talking to beckoned us to follow him through the gate and into the now-empty line for the ride. That's when we started to feel like we were in one of the Harry Potter books that the park was built to emulate.

Our guide turned out to be the supervisor at another Harry Potter ride in the park. While he wasn't involved with the operation of the ride we'd been waiting for, he had been involved in its design and he knew a lot about it. I took some great pictures of the animatronic

Harry Potter scenes—even better than the ones I would have gotten originally since there were no heads blocking the camera's view—while he told us story after story about the creation of the ride.

As we approached the exit, our new friend said, "You know what? I'm on my way back over to my own ride. If you come with me, I can let you on without having to wait in line."

My son and I looked at each other excitedly and immediately said, "That sounds great!"

As we neared the entrance to the other ride, our guide said, "My ride is the only one in this part of the park where guests can visit the control room. Do you want a behind-the-scenes look at how it works?" Did we ever!

There's a chapter in one of the Harry Potter books where Harry wins a vial of a good-luck potion, aptly named *felix felicis* (which means "lucky luck" in Latin). The potion grants the person who consumes it incredible good fortune for a period of time, during which everything will go right for him or her. As our guide continued to offer us ever-more incredible opportunities, we felt like we had just swallowed an entire vial's worth of *felix felicis*!

In the control room, we met the people who operated the ride. We saw the television screens that monitor every aspect of the riders' experience, as well as the mechanisms that control the fire-breathing dragon, the soul-eating dementors, and the heart-pounding broomstick ride. My engineering-minded teenager was completely geeking out at this point, and so was his dad!

As our new friend walked us from the control room to the front of the line, he loaded us up with tickets that would fast-track us to the front of the line for almost any ride in the park. We spent the rest of the day feeling like VIPs as we bypassed line after line. A day that started with torrential rain and a line that was going nowhere turned out to be a day we will both remember for the rest of our lives.

As we were leaving the park, we stopped by the customer service desk to tell them about our day and express our thanks. The customer service representative smiled knowingly as he wrote down our information. He told us that he wasn't surprised by our story at all. He knew the person I was talking about personally and knew him to be someone who enjoyed going out of his way to make the visits to the park extravagant and memorable for the guests.

Lessons Learned

As we returned home from our trip, I reflected on our experience that day at Universal Studios and I realized that our supervisor friend never actually gave us permission to do what I'd originally asked. Of course the two of us couldn't walk through the line by ourselves without being accompanied by a park employee. Imagine the liability! What if we'd stolen something, or vandalized something, or gotten hurt? Instead, he decided to view my question—my disappointment, really—as an opportunity to do something extravagant and surprising. He decided to give a teenage boy and his dad far more than they had asked for or thought they would possibly receive.

It was a great reminder that my calling as a pastor is, in part, to help people move beyond the disappointments in their life and see a different kind of extravagance—the abundant life God offers. It has also prompted me to look harder for opportunities for extravagance in my own life—not necessarily financial extravagance, but extravagances of time, compassion, and thoughtfulness. If I can create the same feeling of joy and delight in someone else that my son felt when he found out we were going to spend a week at the theme parks, or that he and I felt when we found out we were going to get the VIP treatment at Harry Potter, that's already a win. If I can help someone see the connection between that kind of extravagance and the extravagant grace and mercy that God pours out on us every day, that may be the opportunity the Holy Spirit has been waiting for to open up their heart to an extravagance far beyond my ability to provide.

Our trip to Orlando stretched my renewal leave budget. When I calculated the total expense at the end of my renewal leave, I realized that this one week in Florida accounted for over a quarter of what I'd spent over all three months. If money had been tighter and it had not been possible, I still would have had an excellent renewal leave. I'm sure that there are plenty of other trips my son and I could have taken that we would have thoroughly enjoyed. Despite the cost, though, there's no question that the trip to the theme parks was worth it.

As I discovered many times during my renewal leave, God took my plans and turned them into much more than I could have ever expected. When the two of us left home in a hurriedly acquired rental car, I was looking forward to a few days of fun at a fun place with a really fun kid. I got that, for sure, and it alone would have been worth the price. What I didn't anticipate were the incredible conversations with my teenager on the ride to and from Florida about topics that truly mattered, or the lesson about extravagance I learned from a park supervisor who said "yes" when he could have easily said "no." Those two things I wouldn't trade for all the money in the world.

CHAPTER ELEVEN

Retirement Is Treating Them Well

I've known Will and Al since I first began to explore my call to ordained ministry. They are both retired ministers in my denomination. Both of them have walked with me through pivotal moments of my life and ministry offering words of encouragement and advice. I trust their opinions implicitly and trust them to be honest with me about important things.

They also both happen to live in absolutely gorgeous places. Will and his family live in western North Carolina in a house perched on a ridge in the Blue Ridge mountains with a guest cabin across the road. Al and his wife Bev live beside a lake in Kentucky, where they spend their days boating, fishing, and watching osprey and eagles from their back porch.

I knew that if everything worked out right, I could combine some family time in these beautiful locales with some much-needed mentoring time with Will and Al. I pitched them my proposal: I would head to North Carolina a couple days ahead of Julie and the boys and stay in Will's guest cabin. I'd enjoy the peace of the mountains while I read, prayed, and journaled, and Will would come over to the cabin for a while each day for conversations about ministry. Later, Julie and the boys would join me for a few days in the mountains as a family. On the way home from North Carolina, the four of us would drive to Kentucky for some time with Al and Bev. We'd go swimming and boating and enjoy the lake. Julie and the boys would go home before me, and I would spend the final days of my trip talking about ministry with Al. Admittedly, this was not the most fuel-efficient plan, but it sounded like it would be a great renewal leave trip. Will and Al both of readily agreed, and the plans were set.

On the Mountain with Will

I'd never been to Will's mountain retreat and I didn't really know what to expect. I imagined spending my days in a ramshackle cabin with mouse droppings in the corner and rusty water trickling out of the tap—which would have been fine with me. My imagination, however, couldn't have been more wrong! Instead of a shack, I found a two-story cottage built of thick wood timbers and finished in knotty pine. There was a full kitchen and a screened-in porch overlooking one of the most stunning mountain vistas I'd ever seen. The mountains were thick with evergreen trees and dense fog blanketed the valleys. The air was still. I knew the days would pass quickly as I dug deep into theology books and spent time in prayer.

More than anything else, I was looking forward to several days of unstructured quiet time. Between church ministry and fatherhood, I couldn't remember when I'd last taken time just for me, with no agenda and no obligations. The roles of pastor and dad both require being available a lot, and it is part of my personality to make lists and agendas and constantly develop new projects. Here, there were no expectations, no agendas, and no projects. There was just quiet.

When I arrived at Will's place, I spent some time exploring the cabin and looking around outside. Finally, I sat down on one of the rocking chairs on the screened-in porch and just stared across the valley in front of me. I hadn't been that still in a long time. I listened to the silence echoing off the rock walls, dripping off the cabin roof, enveloping my being. It was beautiful. Peaceful. Serene.

Amid the silence and stillness, I began to pray. I hadn't realized the extent to which prayer—genuine prayer—had been absent in my spiritual life until I rediscovered it there in the mountains. Alone in Will's guest cottage, I remembered what it meant to come into God's presence and to open myself up to what God might reveal through prayer. This was not prayer uttered out of need or want, but solely for the purpose of deepening my relationship with God. I was surprised to discover how long it had been since I'd prayed like that. It felt good—like refreshing rain after a long drought.

I suspect I was not the first person Will had hosted who was being reintroduced to God in the stillness of the mountains. Once or twice a day, Will would either knock on the door or holler at me from the edge of walkway leading to the cabin. This would be my indication that it was time for one of our conversations. Over the course of a few days, we covered everything from our shared memories of my college years to the children in our lives (my kids and his grandchildren) to the current state of our denomination.

I've known Will since I was in college. At the time, I was trying to balance the limitless opportunities of being a nineteen-year-old with the much narrower future of a person called to ordained pastoral ministry. I was doing a pretty terrible job at it, so I turned to Will for help organizing my thoughts. We would sit at a table in the student center and Will would listen while I poured out all my confused ideas about faith and the call to ministry. With humor and compassion, he'd ask questions and offer helpful insights to nudge my thoughts in a productive direction.

Years later, as we sat on the front porch of his guest cabin looking out over the mountains as dusk fell, Will told me, "You know, Greg, I never really thought you'd make it as a pastor. You were so nice. Naïve, even. I figured when you encountered some actual church people, they'd eat you alive." This was honest feedback, offered with enough humor to make it easy to receive. It was also an important moment in our conversation, as it created space for me to confess that there had been times when I didn't think I would make it either and to celebrate that I had made it this far.

On my second day in North Carolina, Will hollered from the walkway, "Greg, we're going for a little walk." The "little walk" turned out to be a several-mile hike down (and then back up) the side of the mountain. Will is more than thirty years older than I am, but I'm the one who found myself trying to catch my breath as he kept up running commentary about native North Carolina plants, the effects of a virus on the local hemlock trees, and wisdom from a long and fruitful life in ministry. In the shade of the hemlocks, it felt safe to raise hard topics like fears about ministry, anxieties about the future of the denomination Will and I both love, and the realities of life as a pastor. As always, Will listened without judgement and offered insights from his own experience.

The next day, Julie and the boys arrived to join me. We spent some time with Will and his family, including some of his grandchildren who were of similar ages to our boys, but mostly they gave us space to enjoy the mountains as a family. We made the most of those days! There was a section in a nearby river that had good rafting for a family with a seven-year-old, and we spent a glorious morning whooping and hollering as our raft went careening down rapids, trying not to drop our paddles overboard. Another day, we learned about how to shoot blowguns at a demonstration in a nearby Cherokee village and stopped at a local food truck for some of the best hamburgers any of us have ever eaten. Finally—far too soon—the time came to load up our cars and say goodbye to Will, his family, and the majestic view. With fond memories and deep gratitude for our North Carolina friends, we headed down the mountain and west to Kentucky.

My First Mentor

Al was my first pastor. He was the person who prayed with my parents in the hospital after I was born. He baptized me a few weeks later, and, as far as I know, he has long since forgiven me for spitting up on his robe while he was praying the baptismal prayers over me. Al held an official role as my mentor during the first few years I was in ministry. Unofficially, he has been a mentor in faith and ministry all my life. Al and his wife, Bev, are among the small group of people I would describe as the most influential in my faith journey.

I hadn't seen much of Al since he retired. We would occasionally cross paths at large clergy gatherings and the two of us had worked together on a funeral for a pastor we both knew. From time to time, Al would call me just to ask how I was doing and if my family was well. For the most part, though, he had effectively disappeared from sight.

As it had with Will, retirement had treated Al well. I remembered him as a serious man inclined to wear ties (or at least button-down shirts) and possessing a clever but understated sense of humor. When we arrived in Kentucky, we found that in retirement Al had adopted a style that I can best describe as Jimmy Buffett without the guitar or the margaritas. Al's formerly dark hair, which he had previously maintained in a style you might call "conservative white male American pastor," was now snow-white and feathered back from the front. I later learned this was to accommodate his habit of careening across the lake on his Jet Ski at thirty-plus miles per hour while the wind blows his hair straight back on his head. Al has never been heavy, but in his retirement he's lost even those few I-have-a-desk-job pounds that most ministers end up acquiring over time and replaced them with a slim, athletic build.

Most mornings, Al rides his golf cart over to a nearby subdivision where he checks in on the neighbors and catches up on the latest news. Then, he trades the golf cart for his pontoon boat before cruising down to Nick's Marina to top off the boat's fuel tank and get a snack. He'll spend a while surveying the family of ospreys near the dam or watching kids jump off the rocks before finally heading back home to spend some quality time with Bev and whichever grandchildren might be around that day.

While Will's gift to us was space to enjoy the silence and stillness of the mountains, Al and Bev's gift was to treat us like family coming home. As Al showed us to our room in the basement, he explained, "We've set aside the entire basement for company—for *you*." Bev and Al showered us with love, grace, and hospitality during our entire visit. We spent hours under the clear Kentucky sky, swimming and floating in the water and riding Al's Jet Ski, which Julie and I both agreed went exactly as fast as either of us would ever want to go in anything without a seatbelt and a windshield. The boys hopped on a giant tube pulled behind the Jet Ski, and they hooted and hollered with excitement for the entire ride. Bev and Al also spent time with each of our children individually and prayed with us all as a family. For Julie, who grew up on a lake, the day we spent at Bev and Al's house swimming, boating, and swapping stories was particularly precious.

After Julie and the boys packed up and left for home, Al and I got down to the business of mentoring. Al had prepared several pages of notes filled with thoughts he wanted to share with me, but first he had something more pressing to which he wanted to attend. In an earlier conversation, Al had told me that he noticed how polite our children were, and that he knew this must be the result of our parenting. I had brushed off the compliment with some throw-away comment about being lucky to have good kids. Truthfully, I'd forgotten the conversation altogether. Al, however, had not. "Tell me," he began, "do you believe that everything good is from God?"

"Yes," I replied, "of course."

"When you said that you were lucky to have good kids," he said, "I didn't really understand what you meant by that. Luck just isn't a part of my worldview. I believe that everything good comes from God, so you might consider giving thanks to God for your children rather than crediting them to luck." The point was well made and well taken.

Like my earlier conversations with Will, my conversations with Al over the next few days were something that I will cherish forever. These discussions were more focused than my free-range conversations with Will had been, and they were more specifically focused on the experience of being a pastor in a local church. At one point, I lamented that I had gotten into ministry to tell people about Jesus and help them develop a deeper relationship with God, but that I didn't have as much time as I wanted to do that myself because there were all these other tasks to accomplish connected to the administration of the church.

In response, Al got very serious and said, "You know, I felt the same way when I was a pastor. Then I retired, and all of a sudden I was around non-church people more *and* had more free time. I spend more time now talking to people in one-on-one conversations about Jesus than I did before I retired."

"Isn't it a shame," I remarked, "that it seems like pastors have to retire before they have as much time and opportunity to talk to people about Jesus as they'd like?" We both sat there quietly for a moment, lost in thought. It was a while before either of us said anything again.

In the early years of my ministry, I was surrounded by mentors. Part of this was institutional. I had pastors assigned to me that I was responsible for meeting with and learning from, and denominational training sessions brought me into contact with some of the wisest pastors in the area. There were also a lot of things I just didn't know how to do. I would regularly seek out the advice of pastors who'd been around for a while when I needed to know how to officiate a wedding, what to do when there was conflict in a church, or where to find words of hope in a moment of crisis for the congregation or the community.

As I've gotten further into ministry, these conversations have become less frequent. Some of the pastors who served as my mentors—like Will and Al—have retired. The denominational leadership also trusts me a little more than when I was a new pastor, so they don't feel the need to check up on me as much. More experience has given me more knowledge and skill for the tasks of ministry, so I don't have as many reasons to call others and ask for help. I still have mentors—a retired pastor who helps me think through capital campaigns and visioning processes, a couple who befriended Julie and me early in our ministry and have stayed close ever since—but many of those initial mentor relationships have dropped away over time. The unfortunate result is that I don't get as much regular exposure to the wisdom of other pastors who have been doing this work for longer.

Renewal leave was a perfect time to revisit two of these relationships. In my time with these two wise pastors, I gained more perspective on my own ministry from their experience in the pulpit. Their view of ministry and life have longer frames of reference than mine, and, as retired pastors, they're able to look at ministry from the vantage point of people currently outside of parish ministry. They're not actively living with the pressures of quick decisions and challenging conversations, but they still remember what it was like to be in the middle of it all. I am deeply grateful for the pastors who have gone before me, and who have done the work in different settings but with the same faith and passion for Jesus Christ and his church.

Throughout my ministry, I have also been blessed by the wisdom of lay members in the congregations I've served. One, a hospital administrator, used to ask me if the "story I was telling myself" about a situation that troubled me at the church lined up with the reality of what was going on. Another was a computer programmer who taught himself theology and knew far more about the Bible than I ever will. I remember a married couple in the first church where I served who taught me by example how to be a faithful follower of Jesus even when life seems to be falling apart around you. The older I've gotten, the more I've also come to value the wisdom of younger clergy, whose perspective on life is different than mine and who are more connected with the changing face of ministry in an ever-changing society. I'm thankful for all these sources of wisdom, and I know I'll continue to seek out new insights from various perspectives as I continue in ministry.

At the same time, I will forever be grateful for the time I spent in the mountains of North Carolina and on the shores of a Kentucky lake with two old friends who have known me a very long time, and whom retirement is treating very well indeed.

† † †

Seeking Wisdom

Take some time to think back on the pastors who have helped you at different phases of your life. Think about the pastor who first identified the call to ministry in your life, the pastor who supported you when you were first starting in ministry and making every mistake there was to make, or a pastor from your childhood whose wisdom and care has shaped you throughout your life. Choose one or two that you might like to spend time with during your renewal leave, either to stay with (if you know them well) or to meet for a cup of coffee or lunch. Even if it's been a while since you've seen them, consider reaching out. If it works out, you'll have reconnected with someone who has been important to the person and pastor you've become. If it doesn't work out, then at least you've taken the time to reflect fondly on someone who has helped pave your way to ministry.

CHAPTER TWELVE

A Tent Will Teach You Everything

Every summer when I was growing up, my family would go on a month-long camping trip. We'd clean out the fridge and arrange for the neighbors to feed the dog, then we'd pull out of the driveway in our station wagon and just start driving. We always had a rough idea which states we wanted to visit, but beyond that we didn't have much of a plan at all. If there was a national park along the way, we'd likely spend a few days there hiking and taking advantage of the ranger-led activities. If there was a quirky tourist attraction along the way, we'd probably stop for that too—I'm one of the few people I know who has, for example, been to both Reptile Gardens *and* the Corn Palace more than once. Sometimes, we didn't even follow what little plan we had. One year, we started driving toward Michigan, turned left on a whim and ended up in Utah!

Old Red

In my early years, my family all shared one tent. As my brother and I grew older, though, we wanted more independence and needed—or thought we needed—a little more privacy. Of course, we were also physically getting larger, which made the family tent a little snug for everyone. To accommodate their two growing boys, my parents bought my brother and me a red, two-person tent.

I have fond memories of the adventures my brother and I had in this tent—like the night we spent in Oklahoma with a hatchet next to us, ready to ward off raccoons the size of cocker spaniels that we'd seen sneaking around the campground bathhouse. There was also the night in Alaska when we didn't get back to the campsite until almost one in the morning because we didn't realize that in Alaska the sun shines almost all night during the summer. That little red tent, which saw so much of the United States with us, was an essential part of my life growing up.

I spent the first eighteen years of my life in the small town of Madison, Indiana, living in the same house where my parents still live today. Madison is where I learned to ride a bike, where I had my first kiss, and where I came to faith in Jesus. It's where I told my parents, and then the leadership of my home church, that I believed God was calling me to ordained ministry. It's also where I spent summers during my college years working as a gate guard at the state park just outside of town.

As I planned my renewal leave, it seemed only natural that I would spend a week in Madison, where my life and faith journey began. I planned to spend the mornings with my parents at my childhood home. During the afternoons I'd walk the streets of my hometown, maybe catching a movie in the theater my friends and I used to frequent. I might look up some of my old Sunday school teachers or see if any of my high school friends were in town. In the evenings, I'd sit beside a fire in the campground of the state park watching the stars. Without question, I would camp in the little red tent from my childhood, which I affectionately began referring to as Old Red.

The stark reality that my childhood was many, many years ago hit me like the smell of mildew when I unrolled Old Red at my campsite that first night. When my brother and I had last rolled up the tent, storing it away in my parents' garage before leaving home, it had been crisp, shiny, and brightly colored. It looked like a tent you'd feel confident camping in.

Decades later, Old Red was faded, with little black spots covering the parts that had formerly been shiny. The fabric stuck to itself in places. The stakes had been lost or scavenged for use with another tent long ago. Old Red no longer looked like a tent you'd take with you on a camping trip.

It didn't matter. This was going to happen. I was going to spend a week sleeping in Old Red. I'd made myself a playlist of my favorite songs from high school, and I was fired up about spending the next seven days listening to old tunes while camping out in my childhood tent. A little mildew was not going to stop me! I bought some new tent stakes and told myself that the mildewy smell would go away once it had a chance to air out—which it did, mostly. Unfortunately, there was a bigger problem, and this one would not be so easily fixed: Old Red leaked.

The first two nights at the campground were picture-perfect. The stars were bright in the clear night sky and the campfire flickered softly in the gentle summer wind. The breeze blew through Old Red's windows and cooled me as I drifted off to sleep.

The rain came on the third night just as I was getting ready for bed. I wondered how watertight Old Red would be, so I turned on my flashlight and waited to see what would happen once it had a chance to get good and wet. What happened was that the water from

the *outside* came right on through to the *inside*. It dripped through
the rain fly, beaded on the ceiling, ran down the walls of the tent,
and began to pool in the corners. When the water from the ceiling
merged with the water coming up through the floor, I knew I had
to do something if I didn't want to spend the week soaking wet. I
quickly pulled all of my camping gear except my air mattress out
of the tent and threw it in the back of my car. Then, I took my cell
phone, my flashlight, and Karl Barth's *Epistle to the Romans* and piled
them carefully on the air mattress, praying it was thick enough that
the water wouldn't come up over the sides. Finally, I climbed into Old
Red, zipped the door closed, and laid down on my little air-mattress
island with neither sleeping bag, sheet, nor pillow, grateful that I had
planned this camping trip for August instead of February.

Aside from this rain-soaked excursion, it really was a fantastic
week. I spent each morning with my parents, working with them
to clean out their garage, which was like a giant treasure box with
unexplored nooks and crannies filled with keepsakes and surprises
that hadn't been unearthed for decades. They'd wanted to tackle this
project for a long time, and having me around for a week was the
incentive they needed to actually do it.

It took the entire week, but we got it done. I ended up with a
dart board (with most of the darts still with it!) that would find a
new home in our parsonage basement and a pillowcase my great-
grandmother embroidered that will someday grace a new pillow on
our couch (if I ever learn how to sew it back up around some stuffing). We also located some things I didn't even know existed, like a
plastic tub my mom had stashed away with all the birthday cards my
brother and I had given her along with many of the art projects we'd
brought home from school. The greatest treasures of all, though, were
the stories the discoveries in the garage evoked. An old electric drill

recalled a story about my grandfather, who'd given the drill to my dad when he was a young man. A plywood cutout of a soccer ball was the catalyst for a lengthy conversation about my brother's senior year of high school and the traveling soccer team he played on.

I spent each afternoon that week in town, basking in old memories. I ate a slider at the local greasy spoon where my friends and I used to hang out, coming away wearing that familiar smell of grease and fried onions on my clothes. I made my way down to the riverbank and thought back on the hours I used to spend skipping stones there. I toured some historic homes that I hadn't been to since I was in elementary school and walked through the old abandoned railroad tunnel where my friends and I used to look for bats. I also reconnected with important people from my past including the history teacher who'd instilled a love of learning in me, a good friend I'd known since fourth grade, and some of the saints from my home church.

From Hanover to Main Street

Despite the leaky tent, early mornings and late evenings at the campground were glorious. I watched woodpeckers hunt for beetles in downed trees and made friends with a family of raccoons that lived in the campground. I got to know the staff at the campground and the park naturalists, who helped me catch up on all the things that had changed since I'd worked there a quarter-century before.

Abba Moses, a desert monk from the early centuries of the church, once famously said "Go, sit in your cell, and your cell will teach you everything."[1] For the week I spent in my hometown, am old, mildewy, leaky red tent became my cell. My tent-cell taught me a great deal about silence, about prayer, and about faithful reflection on the past. It also helped me work through a dilemma that had been troubling me.

The church where I grew up, Hanover United Methodist Church, sits on the edge of a small town of about 3,500 people a few miles down the road from my hometown of Madison. There's a small college in the center of the town, and its outskirts are surrounded by corn and bean fields. Farmers and faculty members sit next to each other on the hardwood pews of the church and work side by side on mission trips. My high school Sunday school teacher was a sociology professor at the college, while my junior high Sunday school teacher grew up on a farm and worked at the local power plant. This blend of cultures instilled in me and the other children of the church a rich, diverse spiritual life by combining the no-nonsense faith of folks who know they depend on God for the rain that waters their crops with a passion for the sorts of learning and questioning valued by academics. As an adult and as a pastor, I realize what a unique and wonderful church it is, and how fortunate I was to grow up in it. As a kid, I just thought of it as home.

I remember all the pastors from my childhood years with fondness. The the pastor who came to every youth group activity helped the teens of the church realize how much we mattered to her. The pastor with a particular passion for college ministry filled the pews with students each week. The pastor who peppered his sermons with current cultural references seemed oh-so-relevant to my high

---

1. Benedicta Ward, *The Sayings of the Desert Fathers: The Alphabetical Collection*, (Kalamazoo, MI: Cistercian Publications, 1984), p.139.

school-aged Christian self. There was something particularly special, though, about the pastors who stayed at our church for more than the three or four years that seemed to be typical for pastoral tenures at Hanover UMC.

Longevity matters when it comes to church ministry. Pastors whose work at a church spans six or seven or even ten years are there long enough to explore the nuances of the congregation. They understand the strengths and weaknesses of a church that may not be immediately visible. They've had time to build up trust with the congregation, so they can lead it in making systemic, long-lasting changes. I am thankful for all the pastors who came to our church for any amount of time, and for the way they shaped me. I can also say without a doubt that each pastor's impact on my life and on the church increased the longer she or he was there.

Main Street United Methodist Church, the church to where I am currently appointed, looks out over the town square of Boonville, Indiana, a community of just over 6,000 people. Though farming isn't big in this part of Indiana, coal mining and aluminum smelting are. There are also several colleges and universities in the nearby city of Evansville that are major employers. As I stand before the congregation on Sunday morning, distributing the elements of the sacrament of Communion, I might serve someone who works at the university, then an employee of the nearby aluminum smelter, and then a schoolteacher at one of the elementary schools in town. The congregation's openness to new ideas combined with a straightforward faith in Jesus Christ feels similar to my childhood church in Hanover.

As I was planning my renewal leave, I was also coming up on my five-year anniversary at Main Street. A few years ago, a history-loving member of the church created a timeline for the congregation's 175th anniversary and posted it along the wall in one of the hallways at the church. A look down that timeline shows a similar pattern—two years here, four or five years there—perhaps a little bit longer than the norm at Hanover, but still not many long-term pastorates. I longed to give the congregation at Main Street the gift that I valued so much when I was growing up—the gift of long-term pastoral leadership.

At the same time, though, I was beginning to wonder whether it might be time to move on. As a pastor who had been at the same church for half a decade, I was beginning to get carefully worded inquiries from denominational authorities—not "You have to move," but "If something came up, would you be interested in being considered?" I also knew that several colleagues who had started in ministry around the same time as me were moving to larger churches. I wondered if I'd be missing out on a natural progression if I stayed at Main Street much longer.

Mostly, after five years in ministry in the same place, I was starting to get a familiar itch. United Methodist ministers operate under a system of itinerancy, in which we are appointed to a church for twelve months at a time. We're then reappointed by the denominational leadership every summer—either to the church we are currently serving, or to a new church. Over time, this can create a sort of itinerant wanderlust. Whenever our family arrives at a new church, we always fully unpack our moving boxes . . . but we never throw all the boxes away. After a few years, each spring becomes a kind of guessing game—is this the year we'll get the call telling us to get those boxes back out and pack them up? When that call does eventually come, even though we're sad to be leaving one church behind, there is always a certain excitement in thinking about the next adventure.

The Dilemma

As my renewal leave drew near, I found myself genuinely torn. I felt the Holy Spirit telling me there was more work to be done at Main Street. We'd made substantial progress during the past five years increasing our visibility in the community. We'd built partnerships with other churches in the area, as well as with many community organizations. We'd developed a fruitful ministry to support people in our community who were experiencing food insecurity. We'd increased the number of opportunities at the church for Bible study. There was still more work to be done in each of these areas, and, as a pastor with five years of familiarity with the ministries of the church and five years' worth of trust built up with the congregation, I was the logical pastor to lead them in that continued work.

At the same time, that familiar itinerant wanderlust was stirring. Maybe I'd preached all the good sermons that God had given me for the Main Street congregation. Maybe it was time to learn about a new place, preach to different people, start new ministries, and tackle new challenges. Maybe the Holy Spirit had a fresh adventure waiting for my family and for me—that is, if we were willing to take it.

One of the books I took with me onto my air-mattress island in Old Red was *Under the Unpredictable Plant* by Eugene Peterson. In this book, Peterson compares a pastor's temptation to constantly look toward the next church with the story of Jonah. He explains that the way we sometimes imagine our next church appointment can resemble the way Jonah imagined Tarshish, the city he fled to as he was running away from his call—"a far-off and sometimes idealized port" that represents new and unexplored adventure.[2] Yet, he writes, the church we are currently serving might well be our Nineveh—the place where we are being called by God to minister and preach—even if it doesn't always seem as glamorous or enticing as we imagine our next church appointment could be. Peterson's book is ultimately a meditation on the value of staying put, not constantly looking toward the next pastoral appointment, and instead focusing on the grace that is found in the daily work of helping a congregation be a community of saints committed to God and one another.

Lying awake in Old Red, I spoke with God about the dilemma I was facing. The answer I received was to wait and see. If I returned to the church and found opportunities for productive ministry, I would start to make the case to my denominational leadership for staying in my current appointment. On the other hand, if I came back and found that my three months away had made it clear to the congregation—or to me—that any further meaningful ministry at the church would need to be done by a pastor with different gifts and skills, then I would make a phone call making it clear that I was open to new opportunities if any came up.

I didn't end up making that phone call. I returned from three months of renewal leave with a fresh perspective, new ideas for sermons, and a renewed vision for the church. I had changed during my renewal leave, and Main Street had changed too. The leadership had grown in confidence during the time I'd been away and the whole church had benefited from three months of Pastor Steve's preaching and teaching. Shortly after I returned, we began a

2. Eugene Peterson, *Under the Unpredictable Plant: An Exploration in Vocational Holiness,* (Grand Rapids: William B. Eerdmans Publishing Company, 1992), p. 15.

twenty-year visioning process—looking toward the congregation's 200th anniversary—that we never would have considered before I took my renewal leave.

This, I think, is one of the greatest benefits of renewal leave: the opportunity for pastors to step back and evaluate the fruits of their ministry. Church ministry can be so intense, so relentless, and so focused that there's rarely time to engage in the kind of deep discernment and intentional prayer needed to fully explore the question of whether to stay or move on. As a result, decisions are often made based on the pastor's feelings of fatigue or restlessness, which may be issues that can be addressed by renewal leave instead of a move to a different church. For me, a few months out of the pulpit meant additional years of ministry at a church where God was still calling me to serve.

I've been an itinerant minister long enough to know I won't be able to stay at my current appointment forever. I also know that the people at whatever church I serve next will likely be every bit as wonderful as the people at Main Street UMC. For now, though, my renewal leave—and especially that week camping in the town where I grew up—has afforded me a valuable opportunity to return to the church where I have been appointed with fresh eyes and enthusiasm.

That's a lot of insight from a leaky red tent.

CHAPTER THIRTEEN

The Most Relaxing Porch in the World (and Other Sacred Places)

Julie and I often tell people that my cousin Carol's porch is the most relaxing porch in the world. Located on a side road in a sleepy suburb of Pittsburgh, Carol's front porch is surrounded by evergreens, making it feel like it's walled off from the rest of the world. The furniture is plush and comfortable, with plenty of thick, warm blankets to ward off any chill in the air. Birds flit in and out through the evergreens and neighbors call out greetings as they walk by. Carol's porch is the perfect spot to drink a cup of coffee on a sunny morning or to spend a lazy afternoon lost in a good book.

That front porch also reflects Carol's personality, highlighting a gift for hospitality like few people I've known. From the moment we walk through the front door, Carol blankets us with love, grace, and welcome. Food appears constantly, seemingly out of nowhere. She asks how we've been doing and is genuinely curious to hear the answer. She asks what we think about events in her life and listens intently to our thoughts. Whenever we arrive for a visit, Carol presents us with a carefully considered list of activities she thinks we might like to do while we're in town, but she's also content if we decide that we'd rather just sit on the porch, drink coffee, and talk. When we are there, Carol's friends are our friends, Carol's life is our life, and Carol's house is our house. There was never any doubt that we would include a quick family trip to Pittsburgh as part of my renewal leave plans.

We made the most of our time at Carol's. We talked and we played. We went on adventures around Pittsburgh. We ate . . . and ate . . . and ate. Of course, we spent a whole lot of time sitting—and napping—on Carol's front porch too.

Great-Aunt Martha

Julie and the boys had to return home for work and school sooner than any of us wanted. Instead of heading back with them, though, I struck off in the opposite direction. I planned to spend time in the nearby town of Scottdale, a place my family and I used to visit every year of my childhood for Thanksgiving dinner at my great-aunt Martha's house. Carol inherited her gift of hospitality from my great-aunt, who was Carol's mother and the sister of my paternal grandfather. Each year, when we arrived at her house, Aunt Martha would greet us at the door with a big, gentle hug as she told us how glad she was to see us. From that moment until the moment she waved goodbye to us from her front door, she surrounded us with welcome and love.

Some of my fondest memories took place in Aunt Martha's house, sitting around her dining room table. In the morning, we would all stagger downstairs after a long and restful night's sleep to find her waiting for us at the dining room table with homemade sticky buns and conversation. She sat at that table for most of the morning, keeping us company as we ate our breakfast. Later, when Julie and I were married, we would occasionally visit Aunt Martha for a few days. We'd gather around the dining room table and talk with her until long after dark, listening to stories about her childhood while she played old records on her Victrola.

Aunt Martha's desire to care for other people was inseparable from her faith in Jesus Christ. Sometimes, her faith looked like the love and attention she gave to students and their families during her career as a school secretary. At other times, it looked like hours spent in the church basement making candy to fund various ministries. To me, it looked most like the satisfaction on her face as she watched her family gather around the Thanksgiving table. When I was a kid, I wanted to be like Aunt Martha when I grew up. As an adult, I still do.

My great-aunt was influential in the development of my faith and my call to ministry. Her home was a touchstone, helping me understand that a Christian home should be suffused with prayer and hospitality on the inside and provide a foundation for a life of Christian service beyond its walls. Throughout my early adulthood, while I was exploring the call to ministry, Aunt Martha's handwritten letters grounded me in the family I came from and the faith I proclaimed. As a result, the town where I came to visit her also holds a place of deep significance in my faith journey. I hadn't been back to Scottdale since Aunt Martha died seven years earlier, and I wanted to spend a few days of my renewal leave walking through the town and looking for inspiration.

Frankly, Carol and her siblings had doubts about my plan. They told me that the town had changed since I'd been there last. They said that I'd be surprised by how many storefronts were now closed. They were concerned that the town I remembered was not the town I

would find now. Nevertheless, I would not be dissuaded. I felt Scottdale calling to me, so as Julie and the boys headed home, I put my
overnight bag in the back of Carol's blue sedan (which she gener-
ously let me borrow for this leg of my trip) and headed to my great-
aunt Martha's hometown.

Surprised in Scottdale

If I were to do it over, I would definitely *not* arrive in Scottdale on
Labor Day. There was nothing open—no restaurants, no shops, not
even the library. I also couldn't figure out how to get into the guest
house where I was staying, and nobody came to the door when I
knocked. Finally, I was able to find a decent-looking sandwich at a
gas station and took it to the city park, where I plugged my phone
into an outlet near the Soldier's and Sailor's Monument as I tried to
figure out what to do next.

Eventually, I was able to gain access to the guest house, a recently
restored mansion that had once been owned by the financial officer
of a local mining company. This turned out to be just one of the many
gems I discovered during my stay in Scottdale. Later in my visit, I had
an enlightening conversation with the man who faithfully maintains
the town's railroad depot for the occasional train that passes through.
I met with a local funeral director who helped me locate graves of
my family members in the town cemetery and spoke passionately
about the untapped resource of Scottdale's coal-mining history and
its potential for tourism. I discovered that the public library offered
programs that communities twice Scottdale's size would be proud
of—mahjong clubs, art classes, chess lessons, and more.

I also had a fascinating visit with a young man who had
recently moved to town, quickly got involved in several community

organizations, and developed a deep passion for Scottdale's future. This young community leader moved *to* Scottdale at a time when many other young people were moving *away*. Where others saw decline, he saw the potential for rebirth and new growth. He told me about his hopes for one of the organizations he had become involved with, how he wanted to expand their headquarters and possibly use their existing facility to create another inviting public space. When he showed me this organization's calendar for the coming year, I was astonished by the number and variety of events they had planned. It was clear that this impressive young community leader was profoundly excited about being part of the transformation of this small town.

He also told me that the work was hard at times. It came with expectations that were often too high and budgets that were often too small. Sharing his excitement and vision with the wider community hadn't gone as smoothly as he had imagined. The words of this small-town community leader resonated with my own experience as a pastor in a small town. Revitalization is an easy thing to dream about, but accomplishing it is hard work.

Once, in a conversation with some colleagues who serve larger churches, a fellow pastor shared about a recent project to repave the parking lot at his suburban church. The church leadership decided to only repair the worst part of the lot because that would cost *only* a couple hundred thousand dollars. My friend added, "We could come up with that money without working too hard at it." I was shocked. That amount of money would fund the budget of the church I serve for almost an entire year! It would probably fund the non-profit of my new friend in Scottdale for even longer than that.

I encouraged this young community leader to continue his work of revitalizing this small town that meant so much to both him and to me. In doing so, I realized that I was also affirming my own commitment to ministry in the church I was serving—a church that had both a recent history of decline and tremendous potential for the future. The epiphany I'd had while camping in Old Red was reinforced during my time in Aunt Martha's hometown.

Sacred Spaces and Sacred Memories

During my stay in Scottdale, I also visited several spots that were filled with fond memories. I walked by the fire department where my great-uncle Buck, a volunteer fire fighter, would take my brother and me to sit in the fire trucks and meet his friends. I sat in the park where we held our annual "Turkey Bowl" football game the day after Thanksgiving, when all of us kids were getting restless and looking for something active to do. I also spent time on the street where Aunt Martha lived, surreptitiously trying to get a decent picture of her former home without alarming its current inhabitants.

Toward the end of my time in Scottdale, I visited the cemetery where many of my family members are buried. It's a peaceful place with carefully manicured lawns and a wrought-iron gate that looks out onto acres of cornfield. I was alone in the cemetery, without the company of any other living person. For a while, I sat next to the graves of Aunt Martha, her husband, Buck, and her parents—my great-grandparents. I recalled the smell of Aunt Martha's house when Thanksgiving dinner was almost ready; the sounds of playing football with my cousins along a side street or throwing a tennis ball against the wall of a nearby building; the taste of the homemade chocolates Aunt Martha would pass around as the family talked late into Thanksgiving night. I thought. I prayed. I gave thanks.

Over the course of my days in Scottdale, I was also reading *Kafka on the Shore*, a book written by Japanese author Haruki Murakami. I'd randomly picked it up from the library shelf before my trip. It is not the kind of book I usually read—it's a work of surrealist fiction that is, at times, quite graphic (just a warning in case you decide to read it)—but it gave me an important insight for my renewal leave. At the end of the book, two of the characters are tasked with carrying the memories of someone with whom their life has intersected. One of the characters will go forward in life remembering a man he traveled with for a while who became like a teacher to him. The other is tasked with remembering a person he has loved deeply and passionately.

Walking the streets of Scottdale, this idea of carrying memories resonated with me. I am thankful for the way I have been shaped by those who have gone before me, and I am filled with gratitude when I think about family members like Aunt Martha, mentors like Will and Al, and places like Scottdale and Madison that have been crucial in shaping my faith and my call to ministry. Part of my call as a person is to carry their memories, just as it is part of my call as a pastor to carry the memory of Jesus' disciples and their experience with Him.

Some sacred places in life are universally recognized as such—monasteries, convents, church sanctuaries, and other holy sites. We approach these places with a sense of reverence and awe, and rightly so. Renewal leave gave me the space to explore and re-encounter some of the sacred places from my life. During this trip to my great-aunt Martha's hometown, I was blessed to visit spaces which are no less sacred for being unique to my own life and spiritual growth—places like a front porch where hospitality is embodied and napping is encouraged, a house where sticky buns and Thanksgiving dinner prayers helped shape me into the person of faith I am today, and a graveyard where the mortal remains of one of the most significant saints in my life will rest until Jesus returns and calls her into service. And on that day, all Creation will become a sacred place and God's kingdom will be perfected on earth as it is in heaven.

† † †

Sacred People, Sacred Places

What are some sacred places in your life? Who are some of the sacred people who have influenced your life? Pick one or two people along with one or two places—the people and the places may well be connected—then take some time in the next few days to give thanks for them and to reflect on how they have helped shape you into the person and pastor that you have become. Look through old photos and find pictures of them. If you have videos or other recordings, pull them up and experience them again. If these people are no longer living, call a friend or family member who remembers them as well and talk about them. Consider planning a trip during your renewal leave that will allow you to reconnect with these sacred people and sacred places in your life.

CHAPTER FOURTEEN

Tired of Hearing Myself Talk

I've always loved sermons. I love preaching sermons; I love listening to other people preach. As a teenager, I managed to get myself assigned to preach one of the mini-sermons every year on Youth Sunday. One year, driving home from college at the end of semester, I listened to more than three hours' worth of sermons on the radio and would have listened to more if I'd been able to find any. In seminary, I relished my preaching classes and approached each of them with excitement and passion. In fact, I really can't think of many things I enjoy more than sitting in a church service, listening to a really good sermon.

It's ironic, then, that I picked possibly the *only* job in the world that ensures that I hardly ever get to hear an actual live, in-person sermon preached by someone other than me. While there were a dozen good reasons for me to take renewal leave, this one was quietly close to the top. After fifteen years of ministry, I was starting to get tired of hearing myself talk!

Now, it's not like I *never* got to hear anyone else preach. I listen to sermons online and have heard some fantastic sermons that way. For me, though, there's nothing quite like being in the same space as the preacher and the congregation who are hearing the sermon. While I have four weeks of vacation a year and we generally attend worship somewhere else on those Sundays, we usually pick the churches based on which one is nearest to our campsite or hotel—which is efficient, but means the sermons can be hit-or-miss. After a decade and a half of preparing sermons every week and delivering them every Sunday, I was ready to hear other people preach for a while.

Sunday Mornings with Friends

I highly recommend traveling to hear your friends and colleagues preach as part of your renewal leave. Over the course of the three months I was away from the pulpit, I heard some great sermons. More importantly, I deepened my friendships with the people I went to hear preach.

With that said, I will also admit that it took far more planning and creativity than I'd anticipated to actually accomplish this goal. For one thing, when I looked at my list of friends and colleagues I wanted to hear preach, I was quickly reminded that several of them live hundreds of miles away—and not all in the same direction! To add on an extra layer of complication, my renewal leave was over the summer, when many preachers are taking vacations, leading mission trips, or directing church camps. After lots of emails and phone calls, some schedule adjustments, and the resigned acknowledgement that I simply wasn't going to get to hear certain friends preach, it all came together, and I was ready to listen to three months of excellent sermons.

To my delight, I discovered that many of my friends whom I've always imagined to be good preachers are, in fact, very good preachers! Two of my favorite sermons were given by my friends Isaac and Jen. Each of them has a very different preaching style than I do, and they both preach in a significantly different setting than mine. Despite these differences—or possibly *because* of them—these two sermons provided me with important insights into my own understanding of preaching.

The Country Preacher

Isaac is one of the smartest pastors I know. He has a Ph.D. in theology and a vast storehouse of biblical facts and insights he can access off the top of his head. In addition to being a pastor, he has also taught several seminary-level classes. Isaac could preach a sermon at any seminary in the country, and I'm confident it would be well received. And, as was made clear by the sermon I heard him preach, he's also capable of speaking into a wide variety of settings.

When I heard Isaac preach, he was serving as the pastor of a rural church located several miles outside Fort Wayne, the second-largest city in Indiana. The church was in the middle of a massive renovation, so the worship service was held in the church's gym instead of the sanctuary. It was about what you'd expect from a service in a gym—the acoustics were a disaster, the folding chairs were uncomfortable, and it was hard to see from the back. Not the optimal preaching conditions, to say the least.

But you'd never know that from hearing Isaac preach. He treated that space like it was the Sistine Chapel. Preaching without notes, completely unfazed by his surroundings, Isaac delivered a sermon that was both theologically deep and easily accessible. He grabbed the attention of his congregation and they stayed focused for the entire sermon. The message contained a plethora of facts and insights from that vast storehouse of knowledge in Isaac's head, yet was presented in a way that drew his listeners in and brought us all closer to God.

I often find myself leaving good material out of my sermons because I don't want to risk losing the congregation and not being able to get them back. In many ways, this is a good preaching strategy—nobody wants to hear everything the preacher knows or thinks about a passage of Scripture. When I heard Isaac preach, though, I was challenged to consider whether I might be leaving too much out. His sermon was peppered with the knowledge and details that are an integral part of what he brings to ministry. Because he presented them in a way that was engaging and clear, the congregation was able to take these facts in and connect them to their own lives and faith journeys. Hearing Isaac preach reminded me that learning is not the enemy of clarity for a preacher, and that it is not necessary to choose between *information* and *inspiration*, as though the two were mutually exclusive. It's all about how you present it.

The City Preacher

The setting for Jen's sermon was a study in contrasts with Isaac's church. At the time, Jen was the lead pastor of a large suburban church in Indianapolis. Instead of a makeshift chancel at the front of a church gym, she preached from a raised pulpit in a beautifully decorated sanctuary.

Jen is a second-career pastor who came to ministry from a career in public education administration. She projects a calm, confident style that suggests she's handled far bigger administrative crises than anything she's likely to find in a church. This confidence is paired with a relaxed manner toward her parishioners that makes you suspect Jen finds church folk refreshingly easy to deal with.

On the Sunday when I was in attendance, Jen was part of the way through an all-church study on the book of Ephesians. Her sermon that day was an in-depth examination of the chapter they were currently studying, and she dug deep into the text assigned for that day—parsing it verse by verse and word by word, providing context, and mining the Scripture for truth.

I generally preach in a narrative style, so Jen's expository style felt a bit foreign to me. By the end of the sermon, though, I was ready to give Jen's way a try! After a brief opening story, she launched into a deft exposition of the passage from Ephesians. Throughout the remainder of the sermon, Jen seamlessly wove biblical stories together with stories from the congregation's life. She made surprising and enlightening connections between Paul's context and the congregation's own experience. Listening to the sermon, I knew Jen's parishioners would emerge from this sermon series understanding the book of Ephesians more clearly and having gained a solid framework to live out Paul's teaching in their daily lives.

From my perspective, the sermon series felt like a somewhat risky move. Before hearing Jen preach, I would never have assumed a congregation would embrace a multi-week, full-on Bible study from the pulpit. Small groups during the week, sure. On Sunday morning, though? I would have been afraid to try it. Jen's sermon reminded me that congregations may be open to a wider variety of sermon styles from the pulpit than I might assume. It was a good affirmation that taking risks can create opportunities for congregational growth (and pastoral growth), and it challenged me to be more risk-taking in my choice of sermon topics and styles.

The SermonFeast

When I started planning my renewal leave, I assumed thirteen Sundays would be more than enough time to hear my friends and colleagues preach. When I started writing down a list of people I wanted to hear preach and matching them up with the Sundays of my renewal leave, I realized there were significantly more names on that list than there were Sundays available. To make the most of my time, I planned one entire weekend so that I could hear as many sermons as possible. I began referring to this weekend as my "SermonFeast."

The theory behind "SermonFeast" was simple. Several pastors I wanted to hear were preaching at churches within close proximity of each other. I had checked church websites for service times and had calculated how long it would take to get from one church to the other. I planned to drive up Saturday night and stay in a hotel close to the first church on my list. That would be the first service I would attend the next morning. If I left that church the minute the service ended, I could make it to the second church just in time to hear another sermon. After the benediction at the second church, I'd hop in my car and drive to another part of the city, where I'd join a third worship service right about when the preaching started. If everything went according to plan, I would hear three full sermons at three different churches on one Sunday morning. It was a great plan. What could possibly go wrong?

As it turned out, plenty. I hung around too long talking to the preacher after the first service, which meant I showed up at the second church later than I intended. Thankfully, I arrived only a minute or two into the sermon, so I was still okay.

I was on the way to the third church when everything fell apart. Earlier that morning, unbeknownst to me, construction crews had shut down the section of the highway where the church was located. I drove back and forth trying to find a way onto that road so I could get to the church and hear my friend preach, but it was no use. After about twenty minutes, I gave up. To this day, I don't have any idea how people got to the church that morning! All I know is that I didn't.

In the way that God often uses even failed ideas for good purposes, missing that third service turned out to be a blessing in disguise. In the back of my mind, I'd hoped to connect with another friend in the area. Once I realized I wasn't going to make that third service, I gave her a call. When she answered, she told me she was on her way to take her mom to the hospital. Since I wasn't in church, I was able to pray with her right then when she needed prayers the most. Later, my friend texted to let me know how much it meant to get that phone call and have that prayer in the middle of her crisis. While I was disappointed that I'd missed hearing that third sermon, I was glad I'd had the opportunity to call my friend and be a support during a time when she needed it. Did it all turn out how God intended it to from the beginning? Maybe so.

By the end of my renewal leave, my soul had been refilled by hearing so many good sermons. The creative spark was blazing, and I had some new ideas to try out on my own congregation. I got to spend three months sitting in the pews with my wife and children. Best of all? I got to come back excited to preach again . . . and no longer tired of hearing myself talk.

CHAPTER FIFTEEN

A Road Not Taken

Although I grew up in a small town in Indiana, I spent most of my young adulthood living in various places in the Southeast. After graduating from high school, I moved to North Carolina for college. During my freshman year, an Intro to African American Studies class awakened a desire in me to learn more. The professor, Dr. George C. Wright, was patient with an inquisitive young white student who came in with little knowledge and many questions. Other professors and future classes further opened my eyes to the richness of African American culture and history. I learned how enslaved persons had adopted the best of the Christian faith without allowing white people to hold religion over them like a weapon. I heard the stories of the Freedom Riders during the Civil Rights movement, the protesters at the Edmund Pettis Bridge, and the students at Woolworth's lunch counter. I was inspired when I discovered that North Carolina had once outlawed the holding of slaves by white Quakers due to their practice of purchasing as many enslaved persons as they could afford, with the purpose of giving them papers of manumission and granting them legal freedom.

It was during these classes that I first heard a professor quote Dr. Martin Luther King, Jr.'s observation that Sunday morning in the 1960s was the most segregated time in America. Twenty-five years later, my own experience told me that this was still true. I also heard some of my African American classmates lament that while many white people might claim a desire for reconciliation, those same white people typically expected Black people to initiate the effort *and* make all the subsequent changes in their lives and habits—which was an assumption I uncomfortably recognized in myself. I knew I couldn't change either of those things on a broad scale, but I thought maybe I could work to change some of them in my own life.

With this in mind, when I would move to a new place in my post-college years and begin looking for a new church home, I would seek out a predominantly Black church whenever possible. There were certainly things about me that made me an imperfect fit for southern Black churches—not just the color of my skin, but also some of the customs and assumptions that I brought from my Midwestern, rural, white church upbringing. I made mistakes, asked some dumb questions, and said some ignorant (and surely, in hindsight, offensive) things as I tried to navigate an unfamiliar culture. Still, the parishioners and ministers I encountered in the churches I attended were, by and large, welcoming and forgiving.

Though there were ways in which I clearly didn't fit in a southern Black congregation, there were also parts of me that did. The interactive nature of Black preaching, in which the congregation is actively engaged in the minister's sermon, helped me enter deeply into the biblical narratives and the Gospel message of redemption and deliverance. The Black church's insistence that justice and faith witness are inextricably linked spoke to my long-held conviction that promoting justice should be a necessary requirement of following Jesus.

When I started seminary in Atlanta, I worked to continue growing my relationship with Black churches. I enrolled in the Black
Church Studies certificate program. I signed up for my seminary's
gospel choir, immersing myself in rhythms and harmonies different
from the ones I grew up with in my home church with its predominantly white membership. My seminary internship was at a church
with a predominantly Black congregation. By the time I graduated
from seminary, I'd lived most of my adult life in the South and had
attended and served Black churches for most of my adult years.

As the end of my seminary years drew near, I began having
conversations with denominational leadership in the South about
applying to serve churches in the area. I'd heard that there were some
exciting cross-racial pastoral appointments happening in Mississippi,
and I was thinking hard about taking a closer look there. Most signs
pointed to me spending the rest of my life in the South, deepening my
understanding and involvement in Black churches there and offering
my ministry as a tool that I hoped God would use for reconciliation.

Except that's not what ended up happening. Instead, Julie and
I—now newly married—came back to my home state of Indiana.
There were several reasons for our decision. For one thing, we wanted
to be close to our parents if we had children. Additionally, around the
time that I needed to choose a location for ministry, I had a frustrat-
ing meeting with a supervisory committee in Indiana, in which it
seemed that members of the committee questioned every aspect of
my call to ministry and every significant decision I'd made during
seminary. I left the meeting frustrated and disappointed, stubbornly
declaring to Julie, "The people on that committee *will not* push me
away from ministry in my own state!" Most importantly, it became
clear to both of us, through prayer and reflection, that God was

calling us to ministry in Indiana, regardless of what we might have otherwise imagined for our lives.

We have never regretted the decision to return to Indiana. Julie and I have had a wonderful ministry here. We have had the privilege of ministering to some incredible churches. Indiana is a wonderful place to raise a family, and we have been truly blessed to be within driving distance of both Julie's parents and my own as our children have grown up.

At the same time, I have never stopped missing the South. I miss the pungent, heady scent of magnolias in bloom, the syrupy sensation of sweet tea (made "the right way") cascading down the back of my throat, and the cadences and harmonies of southern Black churches. From time to time, I think back to the choice we made to come back to serve in mostly-rural, mostly-white Indiana and wonder what would have happened if God hadn't called us here.

In my mind, it only made sense that an extended time of renewal and refreshment at the mid-point of my ministry career would include a trip to the South, a trip back to the part of the country that helped me grow into my adulthood and taught me so much. I wasn't looking to test out—a decade and a half later—whether I'd made the right decision to move back to Indiana. I knew I had. I did, however, want to revisit a part of the country that had been important to my pastoral development, and to see what insights it might have to offer me fifteen years after I'd left.

I decided to weave my way through the South, starting up in Chicago then making my way down to the mouth of the Mississippi Delta and back up to Memphis, a city rich in Civil Rights history.

Since it had been on my bucket list for many years to take a trip on Amtrak's *City of New Orleans* railway line, which runs from Chicago to New Orleans, I made that the first leg of my trip. Over the nearly 75 years of its existence, the *City of New Orleans* route has played a vital role in American history, serving in its early years as a route for African Americans leaving the segregated Southern states on their way to the relative freedom of Chicago and the North. Over time, the route has also carved out a place in America's popular culture, serving as the subject of the eponymous song written by Steve Goodman and immortalized by the likes of Willie Nelson and Arlo Guthrie. I had long dreamed of falling asleep in an overnight compartment as the *City of New Orleans* sped through Illinois cornfields and waking up to see the sun rising over the Mississippi Delta.

One of my favorite photographs from my renewal leave is one that I took in Chicago's Union Station. There's a line of passengers standing next to the train, getting ready to board. Some of us are first timers, trying to make sure we understand the conductor's instructions. Others have clearly done this enough that they just want to get on board and start their trip. You can't see me behind the camera, but if you could, you'd see a giddy look on my face.

I splurged on the way down, buying a ticket in a sleeper car for the nineteen-hour overnight trip. Meals were included, so I didn't have to include them separately in my budget or wonder whether my food budget would accommodate the giant fudge brownie offered for dessert. I lingered at my table in the dining car long after I'd finished my meal, watching as the twinkling lights of the Chicago skyline slid by. My sleeper compartment was just big enough to hold two airplane-style seats, facing each other, which converted into a bed for the night. Sleep didn't come easy as I wasn't used to the rocking of the train, but I had put together a playlist for the trip, and my eyes strained to see the moonlit landscape while the melodies of Robert Johnson ("Sweet Home Chicago"), Kenny Rogers ("The Gambler"), Ray Charles ("Let the Good Times Roll"), and, of course, "City of

New Orleans" filled my ears. At last, I fell asleep to the sound of the long, low, mournful whistle of the train.

I awoke the next morning to the sound of screeching train brakes and a bustle of activity in the hallway. I sat up, stretched, and looked out the window. It was just about dawn, and we were pulling into Memphis. I wandered down to the train car door and climbed down the stairs to see a magnificent, shimmering sunrise over the streets of the city. I would return to Memphis in a few days, but for now, my dream of watching the sun come up over the Mississippi Delta had been fulfilled.

The rest of the trip passed quickly as low-country farms gave way to bayous and pelicans. When we arrived in New Orleans, I took one last picture of the sleeping compartment and wistfully pulled the door shut. Then, it was off to the next part of the adventure—a few days in the exciting city of New Orleans. I was ready to *"laissez les bons temps rouler"*—let the good times roll!

I took full advantage of those days in New Orleans. I had beignets, the famous New Orleans doughnuts, for breakfast and dinner. Why not? I was on renewal leave in New Orleans, after all. I heard world-class musicians play Dixieland jazz in music clubs, and then sat on a bench in the touristy Lafayette Square listening to street musicians who could have been playing in concert halls if they lived anywhere else. I strolled among live oaks and Spanish moss outside the New Orleans Museum of Art and sampled what my guidebook said was the best bread pudding in New Orleans. I drank sweet tea with nearly every meal, savoring every sip of the sweet syrupy drink. I loved every minute of my time in the city.

My visit to New Orleans passed faster than I expected, and it was now time to make my way back north to Indiana. Before I left the South and returned home, though, I had one more stop to make. Traveling south from Chicago, I'd stepped out of the train at Memphis just long enough to see the sunrise before continuing my journey to New Orleans. Heading north, Memphis was now my destination—specifically the National Civil Rights Museum.

I took the *City of New Orleans* north from New Orleans to Memphis—just a regular seat this time, no sleeper car. My reading choice for this part of the trip was *Why We Can't Wait* by the Rev. Dr. Martin Luther King, Jr. It had been a while since I'd last read it, and a trip to the National Civil Rights Museum seemed like the perfect occasion to pick it up again. The pages of my journal from this leg of the train ride are filled with quote after quote from the book:

> We sing the freedom songs today for the same reason the slaves sang them, because we too are in bondage and the songs add hope to our determination that "We shall overcome, Black and white together, we shall overcome someday."[1]
>
> Nonviolence is a powerful and just weapon. It is a weapon unique in history, which cuts without wounding and ennobles the man who wields it. It is a sword that heals.[2]

The National Civil Rights Museum, which is housed in the Lorraine Motel where Dr. King was assassinated, chronicles the American Civil Rights movement. It serves as a lasting memorial to Dr. King, and to others who died in the struggle to make our nation a freer and more just place. The museum is also a testament to the witness of the Black church in America at a particular point in our nation's history.

---

1. King, Martin Luther, Jr., *Why We Can't Wait*, p. 61. New York (1964), Penguin Books USA.
2. Ibid, p. 26.

The Black church—and particularly the southern Black church—powered the Civil Rights movement. It is noteworthy how many of the leaders of the Civil Rights movement had the honorific "Reverend" before their names. Spirituals and gospel hymns made up much of the movement's soundtrack. Protest marches that ended up crossing bridges or stopping in front of government buildings often began in church sanctuaries.

The museum is a powerful place to visit. In the circular gallery just past the ticket counter, stories of slave life share wall space with gruesome artifacts from antebellum plantations. Statues of captured African men and women seated in the cramped quarters of a boat while chained together by their necks bear witness to the horrors of the Middle Passage. Flowing lines of text on the floor spell out the reality of slave days: the life expectancy for an adult slave on a sugar plantation; the process of breaking a human being's spirit. It is a sobering and thought-provoking room that is not easily forgotten.

Beyond that first gallery, a maze of exhibits and posters tell the stories of well-known leaders like Dr. King, Fannie Lou Hamer, Rosa Parks, John Lewis, and Ralph Abernathy, along with countless leaders whose stories are told less often but who made similarly important contributions to the Civil Rights movement. Visitors are invited to sit on a replica of a Birmingham bus like the one Ms. Parks refused to move to the back of, stand near statues of striking Memphis sanitation workers, and contemplate a reproduction of the twisted wreckage of the Freedom Riders' bombed-out bus. I wandered through the museum, pondering the courage of those who promoted the cause of civil rights and the hatred that would cause people to commit acts of domestic terrorism like those documented in the museum.

Then, as I turned a corner, the breath suddenly left my lungs. Mahalia Jackson's voice echoed out of a loudspeaker, singing the words she'd sung at Dr. King's funeral:

Through the storm, through the night,
lead me on to the light.
Take my hand, precious Lord,
lead me home.[3]

A sign at the end of the corridor said in capital letters, "Silence and Respect." One wall had been replaced with a plexiglass window, which gave a view to the hotel room where Dr. King was staying when he was assassinated. Everything had been left as it was that day—ashes in the ashtray, an open carton of milk on the table, the bedspread turned down. On the other side of the room was the balcony where Dr. King was shot. I stood silently for a long time and reflected on hate and goodness, courage and loss. I continued to meditate on these ideas, and the National Civil Rights Museum, long after I returned home.

We all give something up when we answer the call to ministry. We all have skills and qualifications that we're not actively using— or at least not using to the extent we expected we would. For some people, that could be a degree in a field outside of ministry. For others who heard the call to ministry in the middle of their life, it may be many years of experience in a different kind of job. For me, it's the knowledge and understanding I gained learning from and worshiping with Black churches, and a passion for participating in racial healing.

---

3. Mahalia Jackson, "Precious Lord, Take My Hand" (vocal performance). Written by Thomas A. Dorsey, 1932.

I firmly believe that nothing is wasted in God's kingdom, and that God can use all our experiences and all our passions for God's good purposes wherever we find ourselves. Standing in the place where Martin Luther King, Jr. was assassinated, I was reminded that before he was a hero, Dr. King was first and foremost a pastor. Pastors are called to the places of deep hurt, deep injustice, and deep wrong in our society—not just to visit parishioners in their homes and pray before church dinners, but also to speak a word of hope, of peace, and of faith in the name of Jesus Christ. We are called to speak clearly about the ways in which our society is broken and in need of healing.

Whether I find myself serving in Albany or Indianapolis, South Carolina or South Bend, I believe that part of my call as a pastor is to be a voice of reconciliation. I may never realize my dream of serving in a cross-cultural appointment in a predominantly African American church (though, who knows? Life is long and unpredictable), but I'll continue to bring that passion and those skills with me wherever I go.

Choices

What are some of the things you gave up when you answered the call to ministry? What are some paths you left when your ministry path took a different direction? Are there any of these that you miss? Write these down on a piece of paper or on a dry-erase board and make sure they are somewhere you will see them often as you are planning your renewal leave. Consider planning a trip or activity during your renewal leave that will reconnect you with one or more of them.

CHAPTER SIXTEEN

Sagebrush, Rattlesnakes, and the Monastery at the End of the World

My wife doesn't often tell me that I *have* to do something. When she does, it's a big deal. That's why I sat up and took notice when Julie told me, "You ABSOLUTELY HAVE to go to the Monastery of Christ in the Desert," as I was planning my renewal leave.

Several years earlier, Julie had spent time at Christ in the Desert as part of a cultural immersion trip her seminary took to Native American lands in the western United States. She had come back . . . different, more centered, more peaceful. She couldn't stop talking about her time at the monastery. I wanted some that peacefulness too, so I decided to take her advice and plan a trip to New Mexico. I wanted to see if I could find what she'd found out there in the desert.

To get to the monastery, I flew to Albuquerque, rented a car, and then drove about forty-five minutes north of Santa Fe. Eventually the paved roads turned into gravel roads—and *that's* when the excitement really started. The following hour was an exhilarating, white-knuckled drive down a washed-out road precariously carved into the side of a mountain. As the road steadily descended into the canyon, I was faced with a choice. Do I take in the astounding desert scenery and risk driving off into the river far below, or do I keep my eyes on the road and miss some of the most beautiful landscape I had ever seen in my life? I mostly chose to keep my eyes on the road, but I have to admit that it wasn't as easy a choice as you might think.

After what seemed like a lifetime of tortuous driving, a wooden sign announced that I'd arrived at the monastery. I parked my car and walked through the wood-slat gate into the adobe guest house. My desert home for the next few days turned out to be a simple cell with a red tiled floor, a small writing desk, a lamp, and a bed with a thick wool blanket. Outside the front door, hardy desert plants filled a central courtyard. From the back window I could see a footpath leading to some unknown destination, along with a clothesline and a small tree growing improbably out of an imposing red sandstone boulder. Printed instructions on the small desk invited me to daily prayers with the monks, so I dropped off my luggage, then made my way along the half-mile gravel pathway to the chapel where the monks pray.

The chapel itself is a simple building of wood timbers and adobe. It's the setting that takes your breath away. The chapel where the monks of Christ in the Desert hold their daily prayers is situated at the bottom of a deep sandstone canyon carved out over milennia by the Chama River. The top third of the chapel wall is made of clear glass, so that a worshiper's eyes are pulled away from the altar to the canyon walls towering over the humble structure. As I took in the view, I thought to myself, "*This* is where I get to pray for the next few days!" and offered thanks for this place God had brought me to. It would be the first of many similar prayers in the days ahead.

I came to Christ in the Desert open to whatever God had in store for me. I also came with a purpose of my own. Over the course of my renewal leave, I'd had the chance to spend time with my family. I'd visited familiar places from my childhood and young adulthood. I'd reconnected with long-time mentors and talked with them about my ministry. Now, at a monastery deep in the middle of the desert, I was hoping to hear a word from God about what might be in store for me in the years ahead.

It is here that I should offer a word of warning, something important I learned at Christ in the Desert: When you're on renewal leave, never ask for something you're not ready to receive!

On my last full day at the monastery, I rose from my bed long before daylight so I could arrive at the chapel in time for the first prayer of the morning. I slipped out of my room quietly to avoid waking the other guests on retreat. Slowly and carefully, I made my way down the path to the chapel, just as I had done each day since I had arrived at the monastery.

But strange things happen in the desert.

This time I didn't make it to the chapel in time for morning prayer. I didn't make it in time for the next set of prayers either. About halfway down the path, I looked up at the sky overhead. The stars were bright and clear in the inky black night. A cool breeze rustled the leaves of the fragrant desert plants. The river lapped at its banks, just barely audible in the distance. There, on the footpath, in the dark, I began to worship God. I quietly sang the doxology, gently offering the words "Praise God from Whom all blessings flow . . ." I sang praise songs and familiar hymns, softly but joyfully. I prayed and praised God under my breath. As the first hint of morning light brushed the sandstone cliffs, the canyon walls became visible. And then suddenly, without warning, my praise transformed into lament.

"You know," I said to myself, "this incredible moment that I've just witnessed happens in this canyon every single morning, but the monks have never seen it happen because they're in that chapel praying every single day!"

The lament grew from there. "If this happens every morning outside the monks' chapel," I asked myself, "who knows what might go on right outside the doors of churches in Indiana every single Sunday morning that I've never seen because I'm inside the church leading worship?"

Finally, the lament became a declaration, a resolution, a tantrum. "I am through! I am finished! I am done being a pastor. I will stand outside the doors of churches in Indiana until I find out what has been going on there all that time that I have been missing over these past fifteen years!"

In my mind, I knew that there wasn't much literally happening outside the door of my church on most mornings, but that wasn't the point. This was a lament about all the things that could have happened, all the things I could have done, and all the things I could have seen had I taken another path that didn't lead to a pulpit on Sunday mornings. This was a lament of choices not made and a version of my life that I had not lived.

In hindsight, I probably should have seen this coming. As my renewal leave progressed, I continued to experience all these things I hadn't realized I'd been missing for the last fifteen years. I got out of the preacher's rhythm of starting next Sunday's sermon as soon as the current one was delivered. I remembered what it was like to sit in the pews with my wife and kids week after week, and it felt good. I got away from the church long enough that I wasn't constantly thinking about this committee meeting or that ministry project. Alongside each of those changes in routine came a tiny voice in the back of my head that said, "This is nice. I think, if I weren't a pastor, I could get used to this."

I realize now that this was my way of processing the pros and cons of a life of ministry. You could call it a test, of sorts. But there in that moment, I was done. I was really, truly done. I was done with ministry, with churches, with being a pastor—and that clearly wouldn't do. My renewal leave was coming to an end in a few short weeks, and the congregation was expecting me to come back, to start preaching again, visiting again, pastoring again.

One of the monks at the monastery, Brother Benedict, was responsible for talking to retreatants and dealing with any problems that might come up. The moment he opened his office for the day, I was there waiting for him. "I'm a United Methodist minister who's having a vocational crisis," I told him. "Are you up for that at 9:00 in the morning?" Brother Benedict leaned back in his chair, studied me for a moment, and then said, "I think we can handle that."

I talked for a while. Brother Benedict listened. I talked some more. He listened some more. Finally, Brother Benedict talked and I was the one who listened. "I don't think you're in a vocational crisis," he said. "I think it's just been a while since you stopped to look around and see the majesty of God reflected in Creation. In fact," he said, "I think it's been a while since you slowed down at all. Once you did, your soul reconnected with God's Spirit, and you're not sure what to do about it."

Then, Brother Benedict gave me a piece of advice that a person is only likely to hear at a monastery in the middle of the desert. "I think," he said, "that you should go and look for rattlesnakes for a while."

He told me about a bridge a couple of miles away, along the road leading out of the canyon. On the other side of the bridge, he said, there was a deserted road with nothing but sagebrush, rocks, and rattlesnakes for miles on end. It would be a good place to walk for a while, talk to God, and sort this all out.

I got as far as the bridge when I sensed the Holy Spirit speaking to me. The bridge crosses a section of the river with rapids, so I sat down to watch and listen. As I sat in the desert stillness above a swirling river deep in a desert canyon, God gave my spirit insight on my predicament. My ministry, up to this point, was the water approaching the bridge from upriver. The highs and lows were in the past. They had already been experienced, already mined for meaning. The ministry God had in store for me was the water heading downstream away from the bridge, with eddies and rapids yet to be discovered, joys yet to be experienced, obstacles yet to be overcome, and meaning yet to be discerned. I felt God asking me, "If I have guided you in your ministry up to this point, why would you think that I would fail to guide you through the ministry that is still ahead?"

I sat there for a while, and then I made a decision on that bridge, a promise to God. In hindsight, I can see that it was the decision my renewal leave had been leading up to the whole time. Perhaps it was the reason God provoked me into taking renewal leave in the first place. There, on a bridge over a river in a desert canyon in New Mexico, I recommitted myself to ministry in whatever way God chose to lead me.

"Two things I know," I said to God. "I am yours, and I am a pastor. Please lead me and help me in my future ministry. I want nothing more than to serve you." It wasn't my most elegant prayer. There were no fancy words or phrases, but it came from the very depths of my heart, and it spoke directly to God's heart.

It was a beautiful and heartfelt moment. So beautiful, in fact, that I decided to commemorate it by finding something to take home with me as a reminder. A rock is a fairly easy thing to find in the desert, so I decided to walk down the abandoned road on the other side of the bridge until I found just the right rock to help me remember my moment of recommitment. It would have to be heavier rock, as ministry is a heavy burden at times. It also needed to be a beautiful rock, as ministry is beautiful at times, too. I imagined myself carrying this rock back to the monastery and bringing it home with me. I would put it on the bookshelf in my office at the church, where it would remind me that I was called to be a pastor and that God would guide me in the ministry that was to come.

I walked for over a mile before I found the right rock. It was smooth, and round, and a distinctive bluish color that contrasted with the reds and browns so prevalent in the canyon. It was the perfect rock to help remember that moment on the bridge.

I broke a bit of a sweat as I carried my newly found rock of recommitment back to the monastery and put it in my car. It was heavier than I imagined, but I had gotten it back to the monastery. In the morning, I would put it in my luggage, and I'd take it home with me to Indiana.

At two in the morning, I woke up with a single thought occupying my mind, "I can't possibly take that rock home with me!" It was at least a foot in diameter, probably weighed fifteen pounds, and I wasn't at all sure I could get it through security at the airport. Would TSA consider it a weapon? I only had a carry-on bag, and I had other things I needed to put in it besides this rock. What would I even do with this giant rock once I got it home? Dust it? Polish it? Set it on a doily?

Ultimately, I didn't take my rock of recommitment home with me. I walked down to the river again and threw it in, then I watched it quickly sink from view. While I no longer had my tangible reminder, the memory of my conversation with God there on that bridge came home with me. It has remained with me and is constantly rekindling my sense of hope as I look into the future at what God has in store for me in the years of ministry to come.

If the Chama River ever dries up someday and you happen to be at the Monastery of Christ in the Desert, look for a big, round, blue rock about three feet away from the riverbank. It will be lying there, a silent witness to the commitment one pastor made to God on a bridge in the desert of New Mexico among the sagebrush and the rattlesnakes.

†††

PART FOUR

The Pastor Returns

CHAPTER SEVENTEEN

All Good Things Must Come to an End

The end of my renewal leave had nearly arrived. Before I returned to church ministry, there was one last trip I had planned—a trip which may have been the most important of all. Julie and I scheduled twenty-four hours for the two of us to get away and debrief after three very full months of renewal leave.

Out of the many people who made my renewal leave possible—all the volunteers who helped the church run smoothly while I was away, all the family members who had offered me a place to stay, all the friends and colleagues who had encouraged me—Julie had done the most, by far. She had carried the largest emotional burden. She had sacrificed her summer schedule to accommodate mine. She had taken care of the kids and kept the house in order while I was away. She had stayed home during the weeks I was off having exciting adventures of my own. And she had done all this while still fulfilling her ministry work as a hospice chaplain. Before my renewal leave ended, I needed to take some undistracted time to tell her exactly how much I appreciated what she had done for me.

In addition to this, I had changed during the past three months in ways that neither of us could fully comprehend at the time. I had learned things about myself that I'd barely had time to process, much less share with Julie. We'd had our own adventures together that we'd never fully gotten the chance to reflect on and reminisce. We had a lot to talk about!

Our twenty-four hours away turned out to be a great trip. We stayed in downtown Louisville, Kentucky, where we could walk to dinner and stroll the city streets. We talked, we listened to each other, we laughed, and we shed a few tears. We ate some great food at a fancier restaurant than we would typically choose while we discussed what life would be like once I got back into the rhythm of church life. It was a wonderful way to end my renewal leave.

Coming Back

Then, just as suddenly as it had begun, my renewal leave came to an end. On Monday, September 17, 2019, I went into the church office for the first time (officially) since I'd started my renewal leave thirteen weeks earlier.

It felt good to be back. Pastor Steve had been using my office on Sunday mornings, so it didn't have the musty feel of a room that's been closed up for months. The dry-erase board on the wall was still pleasantly devoid of tasks to accomplish. The top of the desk was as neat and empty as I had left it three months before. Everything felt organized, fresh, and ready to go.

Knowing that the transition back to church life might be rough, I'd intentionally avoided scheduling much during that first week. I made a list of priorities:

1. Connect with staff and find out how things went over the summer.
2. Check in with key volunteers who had taken on added responsibilities to keep the church running smoothly while I was away.
3. Write a sermon and prepare for Sunday morning worship.
4. Catch up on visits with people from the church who had illnesses or other pastoral needs while I was away.

I figured this would be more than enough for my first week back. Aside from emergencies, anything else would have to wait until the following week.

For the most part, the tasks I'd assigned myself went as I'd expected. I knew it would be good to get back to writing sermons and preparing for worship, and it was. I enjoyed my conversations with parishioners who had been sick or otherwise struggling while I was away. The one big surprise came when I started talking to staff and key volunteers about how things had gone over the summer. I expected a list of challenges they had to overcome because of my renewal leave and things they hadn't been able to accomplish while I was away. As it turned out, I couldn't have been more wrong.

Almost without exception, when I asked what had been hard about the three months I'd been on renewal leave, they said, "Nothing, really." When I asked them what they needed from me to catch up or make up from when I was away, almost all of them said there wasn't anything I needed to do. One of the church's volunteer leaders confessed later that she had racked her brain trying to come up with something. She'd even considered making something up, just so I wouldn't feel like I hadn't been missed! It was almost too good to be true, but the ministries of the church had run smoothly in my absence. The leadership had functioned without me.

When I shared this with clergy friends, several of them asked, "Didn't that make you feel unwanted?" I can understand why they might think so, but it really didn't. We had worked hard to develop a plan. We'd recruited three exceptional leaders for the Renewal Leave Team. We had found an excellent preacher to fill the pulpit, and he'd formed a wonderful bond with the congregation during the months I was away from the church. We had a strong leadership team that was up to the challenge of leading the congregation without mid-week clergy support. Far from making me feel unwanted, I saw it as a positive affirmation of the work we'd done in advance to prepare the church for my time away.

My first Sunday back was a time of celebration. I preached about the importance of Sabbath. Pastor Steve shared a few words of thanks and offered a farewell to the congregation which made us all a little teary-eyed. Before my renewal leave began, I had written a liturgy in four parts:

1. For sending a pastor on renewal leave;
2. For receiving a pulpit supply pastor;
3. For receiving the pastor back from renewal leave; and
4. For releasing the pulpit supply pastor with gratitude.

The first two parts of the liturgy had taken place on consecutive Sundays—the last Sunday before my renewal leave began, and Steve's first Sunday in the Main Street pulpit. We included the last two parts of the liturgy in the worship service on my first Sunday back, which was also Steve's last Sunday preaching. When I was writing this liturgy, I had no idea whether it was what we would need three months later when I returned to the church. As it turned out, it made for a satisfying bookend to the experience for Steve, the congregation, and me.

After the worship service, the congregational leadership had organized a pitch-in dinner and a talent show as both a send-off for Steve and a welcome-back for me. Our church musicians, who typically play traditional hymns during our worship services, had prepared a couple of bluegrass songs complete with washboard, fiddle, and honky-tonk-style piano. Other members of the congregation sang or told jokes. It was a wonderful moment to celebrate the summer, rejoice in our shared sense of community, and look forward to the future. It was also a time to rejoice that God had seen us through a period when no one knew just what the outcome would be, and that God had also brought us through even stronger than we'd been before. I headed home after that first Sunday feeling hopeful and alive. The first week back had been better than I'd dared hope it would be.

Getting Adjusted

The second week didn't go as well. Remember how I limited my calendar for the first week and put everything else off so I could ease back into the rhythms of pastoral life? Well, "everything else" was waiting for me on Monday morning of that second week. I spent the morning coordinating with the church office manager, getting the fall activities and meetings on my calendar, and making lists of things I needed to do so I'd be ready for them. The afternoon was a frantic time filled with phone calls, emails, and getting back into the rhythm of processes that had continued without me.

That evening, Julie and I combined my work calendar, her work calendar, and our family calendar. I could feel myself getting more and more overwhelmed when I suddenly threw my planning calendar across the room and said, "I do not want this back!" Did I mean the calendar, the schedule, or the hectic nature of church life? All of the above. It was not a moment I'm particularly proud of, but it was honest.

Julie just looked at me, raised an eyebrow, and said, "Uh-huh." After sitting and fuming for a minute, I picked up my calendar, and we finished the coordinating conversation we'd been having. Just because I didn't want to take up all those activities and responsibilities again didn't mean I could avoid doing it!

Later, when I sheepishly apologized, Julie told me she knew something like this would happen. She had just been waiting to see when. Julie reminded me how much trouble I'd had the first week of renewal leave—how I'd found excuses to sneak over to the church and had constantly stared out the parsonage window. She confessed that she was glad she'd been working during my first week of renewal leave, because I was nearly unbearable to be around! She told me that she knew the first week back at the church would be just as hard for me as the first week away from it. My wife of sixteen years knew me well enough to predict that I'd have as much trouble coming back off renewal leave as I'd had starting it.

Things eventually settled down as I got back into the rhythm of church life. I didn't throw my calendar anymore. I also found I was a changed pastor in several ways.

First, I had a renewed energy for preaching. I found it much easier to come up with sermon ideas. Several of my parishioners told me that I'd preached some of the best sermons they'd ever heard me give since I'd returned from renewal leave. The weekly onslaught of sermon writing—finishing one sermon and immediately setting my sights on the next—felt less like a burden to bear and more like a challenge to embrace.

Also, I wasn't exhausted all the time. In the year before my renewal leave, most days I would come home and immediately collapse on the couch completely drained of energy. I needed three months to rest, to catch up on sleep, and to remember what it meant to embrace and enjoy sabbath.

Finally, I realized that I needed to slow down a little. I started in ministry as a young adult with very few skills and a whole lot of hustle. Fifteen years later, I had far more skill and competency for ministry than I had when I'd started, but my hustle had diminished as I'd reached middle age.

Making Room

Since my renewal leave, I've been paying more attention to what I've come to refer to as "white spaces."[1] My planning calendar is printed on ordinary, white paper with rows of boxes making up the days of the month. In the past, I took pride in filling those boxes with appointments, visits, meetings, and other obligations as much as I possibly could. Friday, the day I take for Sabbath, was (usually) empty, but the rest of the days were crammed full of obligations.

In retrospect, the problem with this practice is obvious. By filling my days with so much structure, I hadn't left the Holy Spirit any room to set the agenda. There was no space for unexpected ministry opportunities. There was no space for downtime, creativity, experimentation, or play. I'd developed a bad habit of stuffing my life full of things to do, and not leaving enough time to just be.

---

1. I wish I could take credit for this concept, but I can't. I also wish I could remember who first shared it with me, so I could give them credit, but I can't do that, either.

A few weeks after the end of my renewal leave, Julie and I were sitting on the couch watching television after the kids went to bed. I said something about how I felt lazy just sitting around and doing nothing. Julie immediately pushed back, "Nope—we're not using that word anymore."

In her book *Strengthening the Soul of Your Leadership*, Ruth Haley Barton writes:

> Many of us are choosing to live lives that do not set us up to pay attention, to notice those places where God is at work and to ask ourselves what these things mean. We long for a word from the Lord, but somehow we have been suckered into believing that the pace we keep is what leadership requires. We slide inexorably into a way of life that offers little or no opportunity for paying attention and then wonder why we are not hearing from God when we need God most.[2]

Renewal leave helped me realize that the breakneck pace of ministry I was setting along with my lack of attention to Sabbath and prayer wasn't just causing me to be tired, it was also damaging my relationship with my Creator and closing my ears to the one in whom my ministry is supposed to be grounded! In the years since my renewal leave, I've been working on intentionally creating white spaces. When I've found myself considering adding another obligation to my schedule, I ask myself questions like these:

1. "Why am I thinking about doing this?"

---

2. Ruth Haley Barton, *Strengthening the Soul of Your Leadership: Seeking God in the Crucible of Ministry*, 2nd ed. (Downers Grove, IL: InterVarsity Press, 2018), p. 62.

2. "Is it essential?"
3. "Will it bring joy to me or someone else?"
4. "Will it advance the work of God in a way that is more important than what I'm giving up by committing to it?"

I've also been encouraging others to consider taking renewal leave. Now that you've heard about my renewal leave, I hope you'll begin making plans to take one yourself. Yours might not look quite like mine. Your needs and struggles won't be quite the same either. The Holy Spirit's plans for each pastor who takes renewal leave take us all down different paths. However, if you do find that God is calling you to take renewal leave, I pray that you listen and that God uses your time away from the daily work of church ministry to feed your soul, to renew you, and to change you. May God bless you as you continue to work toward renewing your ministry!

CHAPTER EIGHTEEN

Time Marches On (and So Do I)

I finished my renewal leave and returned to active church ministry on September 17, 2019. Just a few months later, in early 2020, news sources across the world began reporting on an extremely contagious virus called COVID-19 that was spreading rapidly through Wuhan province in China. On Tuesday, March 17, 2020—St. Patrick's Day— the leadership of Main Street United Methodist Church made the difficult but necessary decision to close the doors of the church to all but essential workers, to put most of the in-person ministries of the church on hiatus for the indefinite future, and to move to an entirely online ministry while the pandemic raged around us. This began one of the most challenging periods I've ever experienced in my fifteen plus years of ministry.

Several months into the pandemic, I was talking by video chat to one of the leaders of the church. She reflected, "Greg, I was just thinking about your renewal leave. You were so worn-down before you took it, I don't know if you would have had the energy to lead us through this crisis. I'm glad you took it when you did." I agreed with her assessment and said that I was glad, too.

The reality of pastoral ministry is that there will always be another crisis. There will always be another hill to climb and another challenge to lead our congregations through. Hopefully the future doesn't hold another global pandemic in any of our lifetimes, but there will be something. As I think back on my own ministry, I can point to several other crises—a tornado that damaged parishioners' homes and took several community members' lives, an airplane crash that killed four people who were deeply connected with some of my parishioners, the tragic death of a teenager in the church—as moments in my ministry when the congregation I was serving needed their pastor to be fully engaged and ready to guide them through a difficult time with calmness and clarity of purpose. Unfortunately, I know I will encounter more of these crises in the future. So will you.

That's why it's important not to put off taking a renewal leave. If you believe that God is calling you to a time of renewal, a time to refocus and rededicate yourself to your ministry, then listen. If there are people in your life telling you that it's time to consider renewal leave, then listen. If you are reasonably confident that you have the lay leadership and other elements in place to make a renewal leave possible, then why wait?

Start working toward your pastoral renewal leave now. If you have questions or want someone to bounce ideas around with, let me offer myself. You can reach me at greg.pimlott@inumc.org. There are white spaces in my calendar now, so I'll be here.

APPENDIX

Renewal Leave Planning Checklist

❏ Discern whether this is the right time (p. 43)
❏ Talk to someone you trust (p. 27)
❏ Approach key church leaders (p. 28)
❏ Create a Renewal Leave Team at your church (p. 30)
❏ Create an Intervention Team at your church (not essential, but it's a good idea) (p. 30)
❏ Develop a schedule for your renewal leave (p. 53)
❏ Decide where you'll worship (p. 62)
❏ Build your budget (p. 65)
❏ Identify funding sources (p. 66)
❏ Start a reading list (p. 58)
❏ Plan for your return (p. 77)

Renewal Leave Brainstorming Prompts

Use a blank sheet of paper or the space provided to write, draw, or otherwise respond to the following questions. Go back after a few days and highlight the ideas that resonate the most with you.

1. "What am I missing right now in my life and ministry?"
2. "What feeds my soul?"
3. "Who are the most important people in my life?"
4. "What brings me joy?"

A Six-Day Devotion for Your Renewal Leave

You'll find many ways to reconnect with God during your renewal leave, including devotional readings. If you have a daily devotional resource that you're already using, be sure to take it with you wherever you go!

You can also use this six-day set of devotions which I've prepared specifically for clergy who are on renewal leave. To use them, you'll need a Bible and enough time each day to fully engage with each devotion without being rushed. Consider using this set of devotions three times during your renewal leave—at the beginning, in the middle, and at the end—and see if your responses change as your body, mind, and spirit are renewed and restored.

Before you begin these devotions, choose something that you will use as your benediction. This can be something that you speak (like the Lord's Prayer or a favorite passage of scripture) or something that you sing (like a verse from your favorite hymn). Say or sing your benediction out loud to close each devotion.

Day One: Breathe

- Begin with silence. Take deep breaths and still your soul.
- Read Psalm 139:1-18.
- Reflect silently on the scripture.
- Pray:
  For yourself . . .
  For others . . .
  For your renewal leave . . .
- Think about one thing that has happened in the last twenty-four hours that was significant to you. Tell God about it as

though you were telling a friend. Consider telling a significant person in your life about it, too.

- Conclude your time of devotion with the benediction you
have chosen.

Day Two: Reflect

- Begin with silence. Take deep breaths and still your soul.
- Read Ecclesiastes 3:1-8.
- Reflect silently on the scripture.
- Pray:

    For yourself . . .

    For others . . .

    For your renewal leave . . .

- Think back on the last few years of ministry. What are the
moments—good and bad—that come to mind most easily?
Don't judge or evaluate them; just sit with them.
- Conclude your time of devotion with the benediction you
have chosen.

Day Three: Lament

- Begin with silence. Take deep breaths and still your soul.
- Read Psalm 69:1-3.
- Reflect silently on the scripture.
- Pray:

    For yourself . . .

    For others . . .

    For your renewal leave . . .

- Think about the aspects of ministry over the last few years that have been hardest for you. Lift them up to God. Talk to God about them.
- Conclude your time of devotion with the benediction you have chosen.

Day Four: Give Thanks

- Begin with silence. Take deep breaths and still your soul.
- Read Lamentations 3:22-26.
- Reflect silently on the scripture.
- Pray:
  For yourself . . .
  For others . . .
  For your renewal leave . . .
- Think about the aspects of ministry over the last few years that have been the most rewarding or joyful for you. Lift them up to God. Talk to God about them.
- Conclude your time of devotion with the benediction you have chosen.

Day Five: Hope

- Begin with silence. Take deep breaths and still your soul.
- Read Romans 5:1-5.
- Reflect silently on the scripture.
- Pray:
  For yourself . . .
  For others . . .
  For your renewal leave . . .

- Look forward into the future of your ministry. What hopes do you have for the future? What gives you hope about your future ministry?
- Conclude your time of devotion with the benediction you have chosen.

Day Six: Praise

- Begin with silence. Take deep breaths and still your soul.
- Read Psalm 148.
- Reflect silently on the scripture.
- Pray:
  For yourself . . .
  For others . . .
  For your renewal leave . . .
- Spend time praising God. Praise God for life, and for faith. Praise God for your call to discipleship, and your call to ministry. Praise God for being God.
- Conclude your time of devotion with the benediction you have chosen.

Liturgies for the Beginning and End of Your Renewal Leave

1) Liturgy for Sending a Pastor into Renewal Leave

Leader: We give thanks for our pastor. We are grateful for her *[number of years]* of hard work at *[church name]* so far, and for her *[number of years]* of pastoral ministry. We are thankful for this opportunity for *[name]* to rest and reflect, to hear others preach as she preaches to us, to spend time with family and mentors, and to renew her spirit.

Pastor: I give thanks for the congregation of *[church name]*. I am grateful for the *[number of years]* that I have been your pastor so far. I look forward to coming back renewed and refreshed, deepened in knowledge and in spirit, with new ideas and insights to share with you.

Congregation: We give thanks for you, *[name]*! We send you forth into your renewal leave. Rest! Pray! Grow! Learn! Spend time with your family! Spend time with God! And come back with new ideas and insights to share with us. We release you from your duties as our pastor for *[length of renewal leave]*, so that you can take renewal leave.

2) Liturgy for Receiving a Pastor as Pulpit Supply During Renewal Leave

Leader: We give thanks for this opportunity to be pastored by *[name]*—to learn from her sermons, to pray with her and be prayed for by her. We welcome *[name of person providing pulpit supply, and any family members or others who will come with them regularly]* as part of our family of faith while *[pastor's name]* is on renewal leave.

Person Providing Pulpit Supply: I give thanks for the congregation of *[church name]*. I am thankful for the opportunity to preach to you and pray with you, to share in your joys and your sorrows. I look forward to making this congregation home for the *[length of renewal leave] [pastor's name]* is on renewal leave.

Congregation: We give thanks for you, *[name]*! We receive you to preach to us during these *[length of renewal leave]*. Teach us! Pray for us! Share God's Word with us! We receive you *[and any family members or others]* as part of our family of faith while *[pastor's name]* is on renewal leave.

3) Liturgy of Sending a Pastor from Pulpit Supply at the End of a Renewal Leave

Leader: We give thanks for *[name]* and the *[length of time of renewal leave]* she has preached to us. We give thanks for the wisdom she has shared, for the ways we have learned from her and grown, and for the way she *[and any family members or others]* has become part of our church family. We will fondly remember _____ *(fill in something here that happened over the time the person was providing pulpit supply)*.

Person Providing Pulpit Supply: I give thanks for the congregation of *[church name]*! I am thankful for the opportunity to preach to you and grow with you, to _____ and _____ *(insert an item or two that were a part of the person's time at the church)*. I will take with me the memories of your faithfulness to our Creator, and your witness to your community in Jesus' name. I will especially remember *(fill in something that happened over the time the person was providing pulpit supply)*.

Congregation: We give thanks for you, *[name]*! We are grateful for your willingness to fill the pulpit during our pastor's renewal leave. We have been blessed by your wisdom and faith witness. We release you from your duties in our pulpit, but we want you to know you will always be part of our church family. You *[and any family members or others]* are always welcome here!

4) Liturgy of Receiving a Pastor Back from Renewal Leave

Leader: Welcome back, *[pastor's name]*! We give thanks for your time away from us to learn and grow, to rest and pray, to read and hear others preach as you preach to us. We are grateful for the time we have had with *[name of person providing pulpit supply, and any family members or others who came with them regularly]*, to learn from them and grow with them. And we are glad you are back home at *[church name]*!

Pastor: It is good to be home! I give thanks for the congregation of *[church name]*. I look forward to sharing the things I have learned and the insights I have gained. I come back with my faith deepened, rested, and ready for more ministry together with you. I promise not to overwhelm you with ideas! But I am excited to share my ideas and insights with you, because after *[length of renewal leave]* of thinking and praying, I have plenty!

Congregation: Welcome home! We receive you back from renewal leave into active ministry at *[church name]*. We look forward to sharing what we have learned during these three months, and hearing what you have learned on your renewal leave. And we look forward to more ministry together with you.

ACKNOWLEDGEMENTS

Many thanks to my wife, the Rev. Julie Pimlott, for your unwavering love, encouragement, and support as I planned and took renewal leave, then came back and wrote a book about it. Thanks, too, to Michael and Daniel for being wonderful sons who are also a whole lot of fun on trips—both renewal leave and otherwise. The three of you are the best part of my life.

Thank you to my parents, Bob and Alanagh Pimlott, and to my parents-in-law, Denny and Jeri Aenis. Mom and Dad, I am truly blessed to have been born into your family. Denny and Jeri, I am equally blessed to have married into yours. Thanks for being amazing parents to Julie and me, and for being spectacular grandparents to our children.

Thank you to the people of Main Street United Methodist Church, for hearing that I needed to take a break before I shattered and helping me figure out how to do it. Deep gratitude to Rev. Steve Seitz and the Renewal Leave Team of Betty Dillingham, Jill Barnett, and Suzanne Weigel for your leadership of the church while I was on renewal leave.

Thank you to Rev. Mitch Gieselman for encouraging me to consider renewal leave in the first place.

Thank you to the members of my covenant group, David, Jama-
lyn, Lisa, and Mitch—more than colleagues, more than friends. We
have walked together through the highs and lows of ministry, and I
am deeply thankful for you.

Thank you to my first readers, Debbie Bushfield and Dr. Betty
Hart, for helping me shape that first draft into something someone
would want to read.

Thank you to my editor Ben Howard for taking my words and
making them better; to the marketing team of Deborah Arca, Terrell
McTyer, Dylan White, and Lisa Lehr for teaching me how to be an
author and not just someone who wrote a book; to the Rev. Dr. Ron
Bell for sharing advice and wisdom as an experienced author; and to
Michael Stephens for believing in this project from the start.

Thanks to everyone who gave me a bed or couch to crash on
while I was traveling, fed me along the way, or otherwise helped or
encouraged me during my renewal leave.

QUOTES FROM PASTORS WHO HAVE TAKEN RENEWAL LEAVE

"My renewal time strengthened my connection with clergy colleagues and my family. These connections are renewing and encouraging my faith and spirit after a time where I felt discouraged in ministry. I am now ready to trust church people again. I wasn't ready to extend that trust until I remembered how much I am loved by God and people. Through these experiences I have a renewed sense of God's call on my life."

—Rev. Andrea Lantz

"I believe I came back from my renewal leave with more peace about being faithful rather than successful. That was pretty important. It continues, though at times falteringly, to help me keep my balance as I serve."

—Rev. Russ Abe